Computer Vision Projects with OpenCV and Python 3

Six end-to-end projects built using machine learning with OpenCV, Python, and TensorFlow

Matthew Rever

BIRMINGHAM - MUMBAI

Computer Vision Projects with OpenCV and Python 3

Copyright © 2018 Packt Publishing

Commissioning Editor: Amey Varangaonkar
Acquisition Editor: Dayne Castelino
Content Development Editor: Pratik Andrade
Technical Editors: Nilesh Sawakhande, Jovita Alva
Copy Editor: Safis Editing
Project Coordinator: Namrata Swetta
Proofreader: Safis Editing
Indexer: Priyanka Dhadke
Graphics: Jisha Chirayil
Production Coordinator: Jisha Chirayil

First published: December 2018

Production reference: 1241218

Published by Packt Publishing Ltd.
Livery Place
35 Livery Street
Birmingham
B3 2PB, UK.

ISBN 978-1-78995-455-5

www.packtpub.com

`mapt.io`

Mapt is an online digital library that gives you full access to over 5,000 books and videos, as well as industry leading tools to help you plan your personal development and advance your career. For more information, please visit our website.

Why subscribe?

- Spend less time learning and more time coding with practical eBooks and videos from over 4,000 industry professionals
- Improve your learning with Skill Plans built especially for you
- Get a free eBook or video every month
- Mapt is fully searchable
- Copy and paste, print, and bookmark content

Packt.com

Did you know that Packt offers eBook versions of every book published, with PDF and ePub files available? You can upgrade to the eBook version at `www.packt.com` and as a print book customer, you are entitled to a discount on the eBook copy. Get in touch with us at `customercare@packtpub.com` for more details.

At `www.packt.com`, you can also read a collection of free technical articles, sign up for a range of free newsletters, and receive exclusive discounts and offers on Packt books and eBooks.

Contributors

About the author

Matthew Rever is an image processing and computer vision engineer at a major national laboratory. He has years of experience in automating the analysis of complex scientific data, as well as in controlling sophisticated instruments. He has applied computer vision technology to save a great many hours of valuable human labor. He is also enthusiastic about making the latest developments in computer vision accessible to developers of all backgrounds.

Packt is searching for authors like you

If you're interested in becoming an author for Packt, please visit authors.packtpub.com and apply today. We have worked with thousands of developers and tech professionals, just like you, to help them share their insight with the global tech community. You can make a general application, apply for a specific hot topic that we are recruiting an author for, or submit your own idea.

Table of Contents

Preface

In this book, you learn how to leverage the power of Python, OpenCV, and TensorFlow to solve problems in computer vision. Python is the ideal programming language for rapidly prototyping and developing production-grade code for image processing and computer vision, with its robust syntax and wealth of powerful libraries.

This book will be your practical guide to designing and developing production-grade computer vision projects that tackle real-world problems. You will learn how to set up Anaconda Python for the major OSes with cutting-edge third-party libraries for computer vision, and you will learn state-of-the-art techniques of classifying images and finding and identifying humans within videos. You will gain the expertise required to build your own computer vision projects using Python and its associated libraries by the end of this book.

Who this book is for

Python programmers and machine learning developers who wish to build exciting computer vision projects using the power of machine learning and OpenCV will find this book to be useful. The only prerequisite for this book is that you should have a sound knowledge of Python programming.

What this book covers

Chapter 1, *Setting Up an Anaconda Environment*, helps you download and install Python 3 and Anaconda along with their additional libraries, and also discusses the basic concepts of Jupyter Notebook.

Chapter 2, *Image Captioning with TensorFlow*, introduces you to image captioning using the Google Brain im2txt captioning model, which is a pre-defined model. We will also learn the process of retraining the model for our own customized images.

Chapter 3, *Reading License Plates with OpenCV*, introduces you to reading license plates using the plate utility functions. We learn the process of finding the possible candidates for our license plate characters, which is key to reading license plates.

Chapter 4, *Human Pose Estimation with TensorFlow*, introduces you to pose estimation using the DeeperCut algorithm and the pre-defined ArtTrack model. You will learn about single-person and multi-person pose detection, and you'll learn how to retrain the model for images and videos.

Chapter 5, *Handwritten Digit Recognition with scikit-learn and TensorFlow*, helps you acquire and process MNIST digit data. You will learn how to create and train a support vector machine, and also learn about digit classification using TensorFlow.

Chapter 6, *Facial Feature Tracking and Classification with dlib*, helps you detect facial features from images and videos, which helps us carry out facial recognition.

Chapter 7, *Deep Learning Image Classification with TensorFlow*, helps you learn image classification using a pre-trained Inception model. The chapter also teaches you how to retrain the model for customized images.

To get the most out of this book

Some programming experience in Python and its packages, such as TensorFlow, OpenCV, and dlib, will help you get the most out of this book.

A powerful GPU with CUDA support is required to retrain the models.

Download the example code files

You can download the example code files for this book from your account at `www.packt.com`. If you purchased this book elsewhere, you can visit `www.packt.com/support` and register to have the files emailed directly to you.

You can download the code files by following these steps:

1. Log in or register at `www.packt.com`.
2. Select the **SUPPORT** tab.
3. Click on **Code Downloads & Errata**.
4. Enter the name of the book in the **Search** box and follow the onscreen instructions.

Once the file is downloaded, please make sure that you unzip or extract the folder using the latest version of:

- WinRAR/7-Zip for Windows
- Zipeg/iZip/UnRarX for Mac
- 7-Zip/PeaZip for Linux

The code bundle for the book is also hosted on GitHub at `https://github.com/PacktPublishing/Computer-Vision-Projects-with-OpenCV-and-Python-3`. In case there's an update to the code, it will be updated on the existing GitHub repository.

We also have other code bundles from our rich catalog of books and videos available at `https://github.com/PacktPublishing/`. Check them out!

Download the color images

We also provide a PDF file that has color images of the screenshots/diagrams used in this book. You can download it here: `http://www.packtpub.com/sites/default/files/downloads/9781789954555_ColorImages.pdf`.

Conventions used

There are a number of text conventions used throughout this book.

`CodeInText`: Indicates code words in text, database table names, folder names, filenames, file extensions, pathnames, dummy URLs, user input, and Twitter handles. Here is an example: "The `word_counts.txt` file contains a vocabulary list with the number of counts from our trained model, which our image caption generator is going to need."

A block of code is set as follows:

```
testfile = 'test_images/dog.jpeg'

figure()
imshow(imread(testfile))
```

Any command-line input or output is written as follows:

```
conda install -c menpo dlib
```

Bold: Indicates a new term, an important word, or words that you see onscreen. For example, words in menus or dialog boxes appear in the text like this. Here is an example: "Click the **Download** button."

 Warnings or important notes appear like this.

 Tips and tricks appear like this.

Get in touch

Feedback from our readers is always welcome.

General feedback: If you have questions about any aspect of this book, mention the book title in the subject of your message and email us at customercare@packtpub.com.

Errata: Although we have taken every care to ensure the accuracy of our content, mistakes do happen. If you have found a mistake in this book, we would be grateful if you would report this to us. Please visit www.packt.com/submit-errata, selecting your book, clicking on the Errata Submission Form link, and entering the details.

Piracy: If you come across any illegal copies of our works in any form on the Internet, we would be grateful if you would provide us with the location address or website name. Please contact us at copyright@packt.com with a link to the material.

If you are interested in becoming an author: If there is a topic that you have expertise in and you are interested in either writing or contributing to a book, please visit authors.packtpub.com.

Reviews

Please leave a review. Once you have read and used this book, why not leave a review on the site that you purchased it from? Potential readers can then see and use your unbiased opinion to make purchase decisions, we at Packt can understand what you think about our products, and our authors can see your feedback on their book. Thank you!

For more information about Packt, please visit packt.com.

1
Setting Up an Anaconda Environment

Welcome to *Computer Vision Projects with OpenCV and Python 3*. This book is one you might want to check out if you're new to OpenCV, and to computer vision in general.

In this chapter, we will be installing all the required tools that we're going to use in the book. We will be dealing with Python 3, OpenCV, and TensorFlow.

You might be wondering: why should I be using Python 3, and not Python 2? The answer to your question is on Python's own website:

> *"Python 2 is legacy, Python 3 is the present future of the language."*

We are looking to the future here, and if we want to future-proof our code, it's better to use Python 3. If you're using Python 2, some of the code examples here might not run, so we'll install Python 3 and use that for all the projects in the book.

In this chapter, we will cover the following topics:

- Introducing and installing Python and Anaconda
- Installing the additional libraries
- Exploring Jupyter Notebook

Introducing and installing Python and Anaconda

The first thing we need is Python 3. The best way to install this is by downloading Continuum Analytics and the Anaconda distribution.

Anaconda is a fully-featured Python distribution that comes with a lot of packages, including numerical analytics, data science, and computer vision. It's going to make our lives a whole lot easier, because it provides us with libraries that are not present in the base Python distribution.

The best part about Anaconda is that it gives us the `conda` package manager, along with `pip`, which makes it very easy to install external packages for our Python distribution.

Let's get started.

Installing Anaconda

We will begin by setting up our Anaconda and Python distribution, using the following steps:

1. Go to the Anaconda website, using the following link `www.anaconda.com/download`. You should see a landing page that looks similar to the following screenshot:

2. Next, select your OS and download the latest version of the Anaconda distribution, which includes Python 3.7. Click the **Download** button, as shown in the following screenshot:

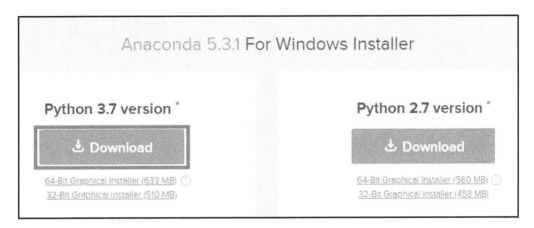

 The installer for Windows is graphical; however, you might need to use a command-line installer for macOS or Linux.

Installing the setup file is pretty straightforward, so we won't go through each step here.

3. When you have everything properly installed and your path variables defined, go to the Command Prompt and make sure everything is good to go by typing the `where python` command. This shows us all the directories in which Python is installed. You should see something similar to the following screenshot:

```
C:\Users\josephs>where python
C:\ProgramData\Anaconda3\python.exe
C:\Users\josephs\AppData\Local\Programs\Python\Python37-32\python.exe
```

As seen in the preceding screenshot, we see that the first instance of Python is in our Anaconda distribution. This means that we can proceed with our Python programs.

In macOS or Linux, the command would be `which python` instead of `where python`.

4. Now, let's make sure we have our other tools. Our first tool will be IPython, which is essentially a command shell for interactive computing in multiple programming languages. We will check it using the `where ipython` command, as shown in the following screenshot:

```
C:\Users\josephs>where ipython
C:\ProgramData\Anaconda3\Scripts\ipython.exe
C:\Users\josephs\AppData\Local\Programs\Python\Python37-32\Scripts\ipython.exe
```

5. The next package we will check is the `pip` tool, which is the Python installer package. We do this with the `where pip` command, as shown in the following screenshot:

```
C:\Users\josephs>where pip
C:\ProgramData\Anaconda3\Scripts\pip.exe
C:\Users\josephs\AppData\Local\Programs\Python\Python37-32\Scripts\pip.exe
```

6. The next tool to check is the `conda` package, which is Anaconda's built-in package manager. This is done using the `where conda` command, as shown in the following screenshot:

```
C:\Users\josephs>where conda
C:\ProgramData\Anaconda3\Library\bin\conda.bat
C:\ProgramData\Anaconda3\Scripts\conda.exe
```

We should be good to go with Python now.

If you run `which python` on macOS or Linux, and it says something such as `user/bin/Python`, that means Python is either not installed or it's not the first thing in our path, so we should modify that as per our system.

In the next section, we're going to cover installing additional libraries such as OpenCV, TensorFlow, dlib, and Tesseract, which will be used for the projects in this book.

Installing additional libraries

All the packages that we will be installing in this section are vital for our upcoming projects. So, let's get started.

Installing OpenCV

To get OpenCV, go to the following link: `anaconda.org/conda-forge/opencv`. Technically, we don't need to access the website to install this package. The site just shows the various versions of OpenCV and all the different systems we can install it on.

Copy and paste the installation command from the site into Command Prompt and then run it, as shown in the following screenshot:

```
C:\Users\josephs>conda install -c conda-forge opencv
Solving environment: done

## Package Plan ##

  environment location: C:\ProgramData\Anaconda3

  added / updated specs:
    - opencv


The following packages will be downloaded:

    package                    |            build
    ---------------------------|-----------------
    conda-4.5.11               |       py36_1000         655 KB  conda-forge
    libopencv-3.4.1            |        h875b8b8_3        37.0 MB
    py-opencv-3.4.1            |     py36h1b0d24d_3         1.5 MB
    certifi-2018.4.16          |           py36_0         143 KB  conda-forge
    opencv-3.4.1               |     py36h6fd60c2_3           9 KB
    ---------------------------------------------------------
                                           Total:        39.3 MB

The following NEW packages will be INSTALLED:
```

The preceding command is a simple, platform-independent way to get OpenCV. There are other methods for getting it; however, using this command ensures that we are installing the latest version.

Installing dlib

We need to install dlib from the Anaconda distribution, similar to OpenCV. Just as with OpenCV, installing dlib is a straightforward process.

Run the following command:

```
conda install -c menpo dlib
```

You will get the following output:

```
C:\Users\josephs>conda install -c menpo dlib
Solving environment: done

## Package Plan ##

  environment location: C:\ProgramData\Anaconda3

  added / updated specs:
    - dlib


The following packages will be downloaded:

    package                    |            build
    ---------------------------|-----------------
    incremental-17.5.0         |           py35_0          25 KB
    werkzeug-0.14.1            |           py35_0         427 KB
    terminado-0.8.1            |           py35_1          21 KB
    packaging-17.1             |           py35_0          34 KB
    astropy-3.0.4              |   py35hfa6e2cd_0         6.6 MB
```

This will take around 10 to 20 seconds to run. If everything goes well, we should be good to go with dlib.

Installing Tesseract

Tesseract is Google's optical character recognition library, and is not natively a Python package. Because of this, there's a Python binding for it that calls the executable, which can then be installed manually.

Go to the GitHub repository for Tesseract, which is found at the following link: `https://github.com/tesseract-ocr/tesseract`.

Scroll down to the *Installing Tesseract* section in the GitHub readme. Here, we are presented with two options:

- Installing it via a pre-built binary package
- Building it from source

We want to install it via the pre-built binary package, so click on that link. We can also build it from source if we want to, but that doesn't really offer any advantages. The Tesseract Wiki explains the steps to install it on various different operating systems.

As we're using Windows, and we want to install a pre-built one, click on the Tesseract at UB Mannheim link, where you will find all the latest setup files. Download the latest setup from the site.

Once downloaded, run the installer or execute the command. However, this is not going to put Tesseract in your path. We need to make sure it is in your path; otherwise, when you call Tesseract from within Python, you're going to get an error message.

So, we need to figure out where Tesseract is and modify our path variable. To do this, type the `where tesseract` command in Command Prompt, as shown in the following screenshot:

Once you have the binary packages, use the `pip` command to apply the Python binding to the packages. Use the following commands:

```
$ pip install tesseract
$ pip install pytesseract
```

We should be good to go with Tesseract now.

Installing TensorFlow

Last but not least, we will install TensorFlow, which is a software library for data flow programming across a range of tasks. It is usually used for machine learning applications such as neural networks.

To install it, go to TensorFlow's website at the following link: `tensorflow.org/install/`. The website contains instructions for all the major operating systems.

As we're using Windows, the installation process is very simple. We just have to run the `pip install tensorflow` command in Command Prompt, as seen in the following screenshot:

```
C:\Users\josephs>pip install tensorflow
Requirement already satisfied: tensorflow in c:\programdata\anaconda3\lib\site-packages (1.12.0)
Requirement already satisfied: protobuf>=3.6.1 in c:\programdata\anaconda3\lib\site-packages (from tensorflow) (3.6.1)
Requirement already satisfied: wheel>=0.26 in c:\programdata\anaconda3\lib\site-packages (from tensorflow) (0.31.1)
Requirement already satisfied: absl-py>=0.1.6 in c:\programdata\anaconda3\lib\site-packages (from tensorflow) (0.4.0)
Requirement already satisfied: grpcio>=1.8.6 in c:\programdata\anaconda3\lib\site-packages (from tensorflow) (1.14.1)
Requirement already satisfied: keras-preprocessing>=1.0.5 in c:\programdata\anaconda3\lib\site-packages (from tensorflo
) (1.0.5)
Requirement already satisfied: six>=1.10.0 in c:\programdata\anaconda3\lib\site-packages (from tensorflow) (1.11.0)
Requirement already satisfied: keras-applications>=1.0.6 in c:\programdata\anaconda3\lib\site-packages (from tensorflow
 (1.0.6)
Requirement already satisfied: astor>=0.6.0 in c:\programdata\anaconda3\lib\site-packages (from tensorflow) (0.7.1)
Requirement already satisfied: gast>=0.2.0 in c:\programdata\anaconda3\lib\site-packages (from tensorflow) (0.2.0)
Requirement already satisfied: numpy>=1.13.3 in c:\programdata\anaconda3\lib\site-packages (from tensorflow) (1.14.3)
Requirement already satisfied: tensorboard<1.13.0,>=1.12.0 in c:\programdata\anaconda3\lib\site-packages (from tensorfl
w) (1.12.0)
Requirement already satisfied: termcolor>=1.1.0 in c:\programdata\anaconda3\lib\site-packages (from tensorflow) (1.1.0)
Requirement already satisfied: setuptools in c:\programdata\anaconda3\lib\site-packages (from protobuf>=3.6.1->tensorfl
w) (39.1.0)
Requirement already satisfied: h5py in c:\programdata\anaconda3\lib\site-packages (from keras-applications>=1.0.6->tens
rflow) (2.7.1)
Requirement already satisfied: markdown>=2.6.8 in c:\programdata\anaconda3\lib\site-packages (from tensorboard<1.13.0,>
1.12.0->tensorflow) (2.6.11)
Requirement already satisfied: werkzeug>=0.11.10 in c:\programdata\anaconda3\lib\site-packages (from tensorboard<1.13.0
>=1.12.0->tensorflow) (0.14.1)
```

As seen in the preceding screenshot, TensorFlow is already installed on the system, so it says that the requirements are satisfied. We should be good to go with TensorFlow now.

Install `tensorflow-hub` using the following command:

```
pip install tensorflow-hub
```

Next, install `tflearn` using the following command:

```
pip install tflearn
```

Finally, Keras is a high-level interface, which can be installed using the following command:

```
pip install keras
```

We have installed OpenCV, TensorFlow, dlib, and Tesseract, so we should be good to go with the tools for our book. Our next step will be exploring Jupyter Notebook, which should be fun!

Exploring Jupyter Notebook

Now that we have our libraries installed, we're ready to get started with Jupyter Notebook. Jupyter Notebook is a really nice way of creating interactive code and widgets. It lets us create interactive presentations with live code and experiment, as we're doing here.

If everything is set up correctly using Anaconda, we should already have Jupyter installed. Let's go ahead and take a look at Jupyter Notebook now.

Open Command Prompt in the directory where your code files are, and then run the `jupyter notebook` command. This will open up a web browser in the directory where the command was executed. This should result in an interface that looks similar to the following screenshot:

Next, open the `.ipynb` file so you can explore the basic functionalities of Jupyter Notebook. Once opened, we should see a page similar to the following screenshot:

As shown, there are blocks (called *cells*) where we can put in Python commands and Python code. We can also enter other commands, also known as *magic commands*, which are not part of Python per se, but allow us to do nice things within Jupyter or IPython (an interactive shell for Python). The % at the beginning means that the command is a magic command.

The biggest advantage here is that we can execute individual lines of code, instead of having to type out the entire code block in one go.

If you're new to Jupyter Notebook, go to the following link: `https://www.cheatography.com/weidadeyue/cheat-sheets/jupyter-notebook/`. Here, they list Jupyter Notebook keyboard shortcuts, which can be really useful for quick code testing.

Let's go through some of the commands seen in the preceding screenshot, and see what they do, as follows:

1. The `%pylab notebook` command, as seen in the first cell, imports a lot of very useful and common libraries, particularly NumPy and PyPlot, without us needing to explicitly call the import commands. It also sets up a Notebook easily.

2. Also in the first cell, we assign the directory that we will be working from, as follows:

   ```
   %cd C:\Users\<user_name>\Documents\<Folder_name>\Section1-
   Getting_started
   ```

   This results in the following output:

   ```
   %cd C:\Users\mrever\Documents\packt_CV\Section1-Getting_started

   Populating the interactive namespace from numpy and matplotlib
   C:\Users\mrever\Documents\packt_CV\Section1-Getting_started
   ```

   So far, so good!

3. The following cell shows how to import our libraries. We're going to import OpenCV, TensorFlow, dlib, and Tesseract, just to make sure that everything is working and that there aren't any nasty surprises. This is done using the following code block:

   ```
   import cv2
   import tensorflow as tf
   import dlib
   import pytesseract as ptess
   ```

   If you get an error message here, redo the installation of the libraries, following the instructions carefully. Sometimes things do go wrong, depending on our system.

4. The third cell in the screenshot contains the command for importing the graph module in TensorFlow. This can come in handy for getting help on a function from within the Notebook, as follows:

   ```
   tf.Graph?
   ```

We will discuss this function in `Chapter 7`, *Deep Learning Image Classification with TensorFlow*.

5. Another neat thing about Jupyter Notebooks is that we can run shell commands right in the cell. As seen in the fourth cell in the screenshot (repeated here), the `ls` command shows us all the files in the directory we are working from:

```
In [4]:  #We can run shell commands here too--very handy!
         !ls

         Megamind.avi
         Megamind.mp4
         Packt_CV_w_Python3_Getting_Started_with_Jupyter_notebooks.ipynb
         butterfly.jpg
```

6. In this book, we'll be working with a lot of images, so we'll want to see the images right in the Notebook. Use the `imread()` function to read the image file from your directory. After that, your next step is to create a `figure()` widget to display the image. Finally, use the `imshow()` function to actually display the image.

This entire process is summarized in the following screenshot:

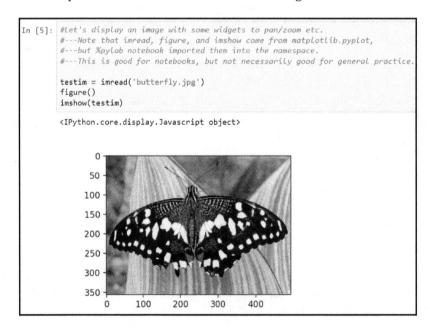

This is awesome, because we have widgets that are flexible.

7. By grabbing the bottom-right corner, we can shrink this to a reasonable size to see our color image with pixel axes displayed. We also have the pan option available. By clicking on it, we can pan our image and box zoom it. Hitting the home button resets the original view.

   We will want take a look at our images, and processed images and so forth—as seen previously, this is a very handy and simple way to do it. We can also use PyLab inline, which is useful for certain things, as we'll see.

8. As we know, part of computer vision is working with videos. To play videos within the notebook, we need to import some libraries and use IPython's HTML capability, as shown in the following screenshot:

```
In [7]:  #Here's a nice way to watch a video within the notebook--will be useful
         # when we want to work with videos
         import io
         import base64
         from IPython.display import HTML

         def playvideo(filename):
             video = io.open(filename, 'r+b').read()
             encoded = base64.b64encode(video)
             return HTML(data='''<video alt="test" controls>
                         <source src="data:video/mp4;base64,{0}" type="video/mp4"/>
                     </video>'''.format(encoded.decode('ascii')))
```

Essentially, we're using our web browser's capability to play back videos. So, it's not really Python that's doing it, but our web browser, which enables interactivity between Jupyter Notebook and our browser.

Here, we defined the `playvideo()` function, which takes the video filename as an input and returns an HTML object with our video.

9. Execute the following command on Jupyter to play the *Megamind* video. It's just a clip of the movie *Megamind*, which (for some reason) comes with OpenCV if we download all the source code:

   ```
   playvideo(' ./Megamind.mp4')
   ```

10. You will see a black box, and if you scroll down, you'll find a play button. Hit this and the movie will play, as seen in the following screenshot:

This can be used to play our own videos. All you have to do is point the command to the video that you want to play.

Once you have all this running, you should be in good shape to run the projects that we're going to take a look at in the coming chapters.

Summary

In this chapter, we learned about the Anaconda distribution and different ways to install Python. We learned how to set up Python using the Anaconda distribution.

Next, we looked at how to install various libraries in Anaconda, to make it easier for us to run various programs. Finally, we learned the basics of Jupyter Notebook and how it works.

In the next chapter, Chapter 2, *Image Captioning with TensorFlow*, we will look at how to carry out image captioning using TensorFlow.

2
Image Captioning with TensorFlow

Primarily, this chapter will provide a brief overview of creating a detailed English language description of an image. Using the image captioning model based on TensorFlow, we will be able to replace a single word or compound words/phrases with detailed captions that perfectly describe the image. We will first use a pre-trained model for image captioning and then retrain the model from scratch to run on a set of images.

In this chapter, we will cover the following:

- Image captioning introduction
- Google Brain im2txt captioning model
- Running our captioning code in Jupyter
- Retraining the model

Technical requirements

Along with knowledge of Python, the basics of image processing, and computer vision, we will need the following Python libraries:

- NumPy
- Matplotlib

The codes used in the chapter have been added to the following GitHub repository:
`https://github.com/PacktPublishing/Computer-Vision-Projects-with-OpenCV-and-Python-3`

Introduction to image captioning

Image captioning is a process in which textual description is generated based on an image. To better understand image captioning, we need to first differentiate it from image classification.

Difference between image classification and image captioning

Image classification is a relatively simple process that only tells us what is in an image. For example, if there is a boy on a bike, image classification will not give us a description; it will just provide the result as **boy** or **bike**. Image classification can tell us whether there is a woman or a dog in the image, or an action, such as snowboarding. This is not a desirable result as there is no description of what exactly is going on in the image.

The following is the result we get using image classification:

Comparatively, image captioning will provide a result with a description. For the preceding example, the result of image captioning would be **a boy riding on a bike** or **a man is snowboarding**. This could be useful for generating content for a book or maybe helping the hearing or visually impaired.

The following is the result we get using image captioning:

However, this is considerably more challenging as conventional neural networks are powerful, but they're not very compatible with sequential data. Sequential data is where we have data that's coming in an order and that order actually matters. In audio or video, we have words coming in a sequential order; jumbling the words might change the meaning of the sentence or just make it complete gibberish.

Recurrent neural networks with long short-term memory

As powerful as **convolutional neural networks** (**CNNs**) are, they don't handle sequential data so well; however, they are great for non-sequential tasks, such as image classification.

How CNNs work is shown in the following diagram:

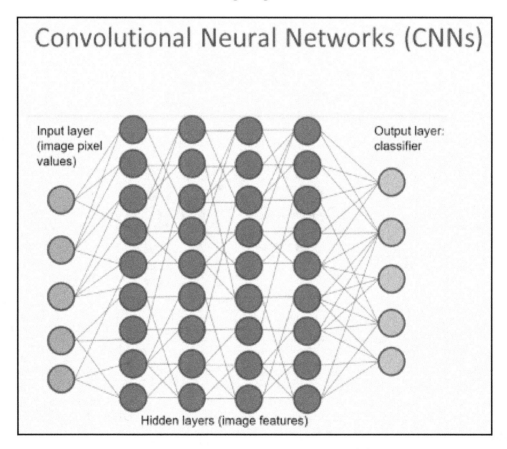

Recurrent neural networks (**RNNs**), which really are state of the art, can handle sequential tasks. An RNN consists of CNNs where data is received in a sequence.

How RNNs work is shown in the following diagram:

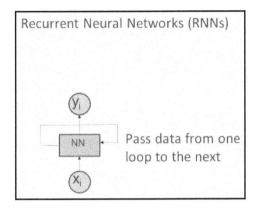

Data coming in a sequence (x_i) goes through the neural network and we get an output (y_i). The output is then fed through to another iteration and forms a loop. This helps us remember the data coming from before and is helpful for sequential data tasks such as audio and speech recognition, language translation, video identification, and text generation.

Another concept that has been around for a while and is very helpful is **long short-term memory** (**LSTM**) with RNNs. It is a way to handle long-term memory and avoid just passing data from one iteration to the next. It handles the data from the iterations in a robust way and it allows us to effectively train RNNs.

Google Brain im2txt captioning model

Google Brain im2txt was used by Google in a paper *2015 MSCOCO Image Captioning Challenge,* and will form the foundation of the image captioning code that we will implement in our project.

The Google's GitHub TensorFlow page can be found at `https://github.com/tensorflow/models/tree/master/research/im2txt`.

In the research directory, we will find the `im2txt` file, which was used by Google in the paper, *2015 MSCOCO Image Captioning Challenge,* which is available for free at `https://arxiv.org/abs/1609.06647`. It covers RNNs, LSTM, and fundamental algorithms in detail.

We can check how CNNs are used for image classification and also learn how to use the LSTM RNNs for actually generating sequential caption outputs.

We can download the code from the GitHub link; however, it has not been set up to run easily as it does not include a pre-trained model, so we may face some challenges. We have provided you with a pre-trained model to avoid training an image classifier from scratch, since it is a time-consuming process. There have been some modifications made to the code that will make the code easy to run on a Jupyter Notebook or to incorporate in your own projects. The pre-trained model is very quick to learn using just a CPU. The same code without a pre-trained model might actually take weeks to learn, even on a good GPU.

Running the captioning code on Jupyter

Let's now run our own version of the code on a Jupyter Notebook. We can start up own own Jupyter Notebook and load the `Section_1-Tensorflow_Image_Captioning.ipynb` file from the GitHub repository (`https://github.com/PacktPublishing/Computer-Vision-Projects-with-OpenCV-and-Python-3/blob/master/Chapter01/Section_1-Tensorflow_Image_Captioning.ipynb`).

Once we load the file on a Jupyter Notebook, it will look something like this:

In the first part, we are going to load some essential libraries, including `math`, `os`, and `tensorflow`. We will also use our handy utility function, `%pylab inline`, to easily read and display images within the Notebook.

Select the first code block:

```
# load essential libraries
import math
import os

import tensorflow as tf

%pylab inline
```

When we hit *Ctrl + Enter* to execute the code in the cell, we will get the following output:

```
# load essential libraries
import math
import os

import tensorflow as tf

%pylab inline

Populating the interactive namespace from numpy and matplotlib
```

We need to now load the TensorFlow/Google Brain base code, which we can get from `https://github.com/PacktPublishing/Computer-Vision-Projects-with-OpenCV-and-Python-3`.

There are multiple utility functions, but we will be using and executing only a few of them in our example:

```
# load Tensorflow/Google Brain base code
# https://github.com/tensorflow/models/tree/master/research/im2txt

from im2txt import configuration
from im2txt import inference_wrapper
from im2txt.inference_utils import caption_generator
from im2txt.inference_utils import vocabulary
```

We need to tell our function where to find the trained model and vocabulary:

```
# tell our function where to find the trained model and vocabulary
checkpoint_path = './model'
vocab_file = './model/word_counts.txt'
```

The code for the trained model and vocabulary have been added in the GitHub repository, and you can access it from this link:

```
https://github.com/PacktPublishing/Computer-Vision-Projects-with-OpenCV-and-Python-3
```

The folder contains `checkpoint`, `word_counts.txt`, and the pre-trained model. We need to make sure that we use these files and avoid using other outdated files that might not be compatible with the latest version of TensorFlow. The `word_counts.txt` file contains a vocabulary list with the number of counts from our trained model, which our image caption generator is going to need.

Once these steps have been completed, we can look at our `main` function, which will generate the captions for us. The function can take an input as a string of input files (comma separated) or could be just one file that we want to process.
The verbosity is set to `tf.logging.FATAL` out of the different logging levels available, as it will tell us whether something has gone really wrong:

```
# this is the function we'll call to produce our captions
#    given input file name(s) -- separate file names by a ,
#                                if more than one
tf.logging.
def gen_ca DEBUG
    # only debug                    ges
    tf.log ERROR                    jging.FATAL)
    # load error
    g = tf FATAL
    with g fatal
        mo flush                    InferenceWrapper()
        re get_verbosity            raph_from_config(configuration.ModelConfig(),
           INFO                                    checkpoint_path)
    g.fina info
```

In the initial part of the main code, we perform the following steps:

1. Set the verbosity level to `tf.logging.FATAL`.
2. Load our pre-trained model.
3. Load the inference wrapper from our utility file provided by Google.
4. Load our pre-trained model from the `checkpoint` path that we established in the previous cell.
5. Run the `finalize` function:

```
# this is the function we'll call to produce our captions
# given input file name(s) -- separate file names by a,
# if more than one
```

```
def gen_caption(input_files):
    # only print serious log messages
    tf.logging.set_verbosity(tf.logging.FATAL)
    # load our pretrained model
    g = tf.Graph()
    with g.as_default():
        model = inference_wrapper.InferenceWrapper()
        restore_fn =
model.build_graph_from_config(configuration.ModelConfig(),
                                                  checkpoint_path)
    g.finalize()
```

6. Load the vocabulary file again from the cell that we previously ran:

```
# Create the vocabulary.
vocab = vocabulary.Vocabulary(vocab_file)
```

7. Pre-process the filenames:

```
filenames = []
for file_pattern in input_files.split(","):
```

8. Perform the Glob action:

```
filenames.extend(tf.gfile.Glob(file_pattern))
```

9. Create a list of filenames so you can know on which file the image caption generator is running:

```
tf.logging.info("Running caption generation on %d files
matching %s",
                len(filenames), input_files)
```

10. Create a session. We need to use the restore function since we are using a pre-trained model:

```
with tf.Session(graph=g) as sess:
    # Load the model from checkpoint.
    restore_fn(sess)
```

The code for these steps is included here:

```
# this is the function we'll call to produce our captions
# given input file name(s) -- separate file names by a,
# if more than one

def gen_caption(input_files):
    # only print serious log messages
```

```
tf.logging.set_verbosity(tf.logging.FATAL)
# load our pretrained model
g = tf.Graph()
with g.as_default():
    model = inference_wrapper.InferenceWrapper()
    restore_fn =
model.build_graph_from_config(configuration.ModelConfig(),
                                            checkpoint_path)
    g.finalize()

# Create the vocabulary.
vocab = vocabulary.Vocabulary(vocab_file)

filenames = []
for file_pattern in input_files.split(","):
    filenames.extend(tf.gfile.Glob(file_pattern))
tf.logging.info("Running caption generation on %d files matching %s",
                len(filenames), input_files)

with tf.Session(graph=g) as sess:
    # Load the model from checkpoint.
    restore_fn(sess)
```

We now move to the second half of the main code. Once the session has been restored, we perform the following steps:

1. Load `caption_generator` from our model and the vocabulary stored in an object called `generator`:

   ```
   generator = caption_generator.CaptionGenerator(model, vocab)
   ```

2. Make a caption list:

   ```
   captionlist = []
   ```

3. Iterate the files and load them in the generator called `beam_search` to analyze the image:

   ```
   for filename in filenames:
       with tf.gfile.GFile(filename, "rb") as f:
           image = f.read()
       captions = generator.beam_search(sess, image)
   ```

4. Print the captions:

   ```
   print("Captions for image %s:" % os.path.basename(filename))
   ```

5. Iterate to create multiple captions with the iteration already set for the model:

```
for i, caption in enumerate(captions):
    # Ignore begin and end words.
    sentence = [vocab.id_to_word(w) for w in
caption.sentence[1:-1]]
    sentence = " ".join(sentence)
    print(" %d) %s (p=%f)" % (i, sentence,
math.exp(caption.logprob)))
    captionlist.append(sentence)
```

6. Return `captionlist`:

```
return captionlist
```

Run the code to generate the function.

See the following code block for the complete code:

```
# Prepare the caption generator. Here we are implicitly using the
default
# beam search parameters. See caption_generator.py for a description of
the
# available beam search parameters.
    generator = caption_generator.CaptionGenerator(model, vocab)
    captionlist = []

    for filename in filenames:
        with tf.gfile.GFile(filename, "rb") as f:
            image = f.read()
        captions = generator.beam_search(sess, image)
        print("Captions for image %s:" % os.path.basename(filename))
        for i, caption in enumerate(captions):
            # Ignore begin and end words.
            sentence = [vocab.id_to_word(w) for w in
caption.sentence[1:-1]]
            sentence = " ".join(sentence)
            print(" %d) %s (p=%f)" % (i, sentence,
math.exp(caption.logprob)))
            captionlist.append(sentence)
    return captionlist
```

In the next code block, we will execute the code on sample stock photos from a `test` folder. The code will create a figure, show it, and then run the caption generator. We can then display the output using the `print` statement.

The following is the code we use to select the image for computation:

```
testfile = 'test_images/dog.jpeg'

figure()
imshow(imread(testfile))

capts = gen_caption(testfile)
```

When we run our first test image, `dog.jpeg`, we get the following output:

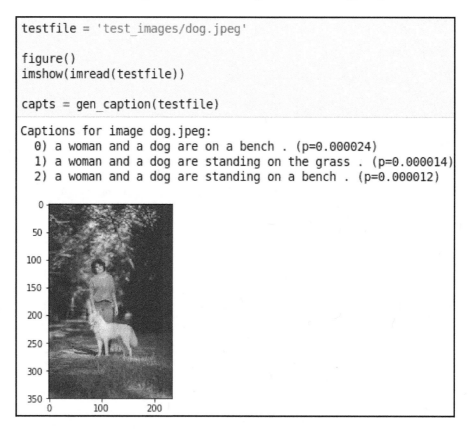

The result, `a woman and a dog are standing on the grass`, is a good caption for the image. Since all the three results are pretty similar, we can say that our model is working pretty well.

Analyzing the result captions

Let's take a few examples to check our model. When we execute `football.jpeg`, we get the following output:

```
testfile = 'test_images/football.jpeg'

figure()
imshow(imread(testfile))

capts = gen_caption(testfile)

Captions for image football.jpeg:
  0) a couple of men playing a game of frisbee . (p=0.001167)
  1) a couple of men playing a game of football . (p=0.001053)
  2) a couple of men playing a game of soccer . (p=0.000807)
```

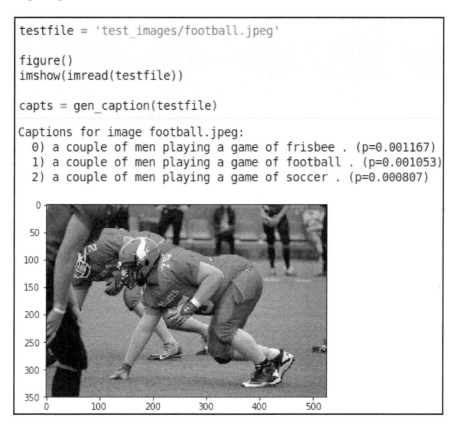

Here we clearly have American football going on in the image, and `a couple of men playing a game of football` is a very good result. However, the first result, `a couple of men playing a game of frisbee`, is not the desired output, nor is `a couple of men playing a game of soccer`. So, in this case, the second caption is generally going to be the best, but it is not always going to be perfect, depending on the log probability.

Let's try one more example, `giraffes.jpeg`:

```
testfile = 'test_images/giraffes.jpeg'

figure()
imshow(imread(testfile))

capts = gen_caption(testfile)

Captions for image giraffes.jpeg:
  0) a group of giraffe standing next to each other . (p=0.002270)
  1) a group of giraffes are standing in a field (p=0.000959)
  2) a group of giraffe standing next to each other on a field . (p=0.000744)
```

Clearly, we have an image of giraffes, and the first caption, `a group of giraffe standing next to each other`, seems to be correct, except for the grammar issue. The other two results are `a group of giraffes are standing in a field` and `a group of giraffe standing next to each other on a field`.

Let's take a look at one more example, `headphones.jpeg`:

```
testfile = 'test_images/headphones.jpeg'

figure()
imshow(imread(testfile))

capts = gen_caption(testfile)
```

```
Captions for image headphones.jpeg:
  0) a woman holding a cell phone in her hand . (p=0.002533)
  1) a woman holding a cell phone up to her ear . (p=0.002143)
  2) a woman holding a cell phone in her hands . (p=0.001198)
```

Here we selected `headphones.jpeg`, but the results did not include headphones as an output. The result was `a woman holding a cell phone in her hand`, which is a good result. The second result, `a woman holding a cell phone up to her ear`, is technically incorrect, but these are some good captions overall.

Let's take one last example, `ballons.jpeg`. When we run the image, we get the following output:

```
testfile = 'test_images/ballons.jpeg'

figure()
imshow(imread(testfile))

capts = gen_caption(testfile)
```
```
Captions for image ballons.jpeg:
  0) a woman standing on a beach flying a kite . (p=0.004793)
  1) a woman is flying a kite on the beach . (p=0.003442)
  2) a young girl flying a kite on a beach . (p=0.002200)
```

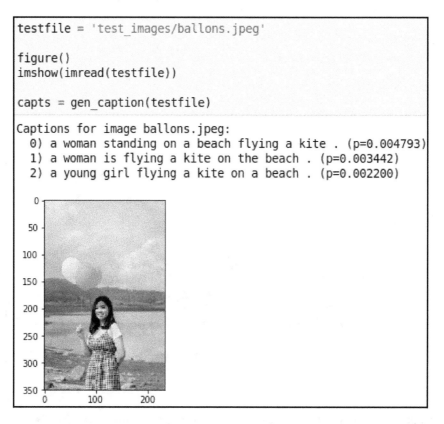

The results we get for this image are a woman standing on a beach flying a kite, a woman is flying a kite on the beach, and a young girl flying a kite on a beach. So, the model got the woman or a young girl, but it got a kite instead of the balloon, even though "balloon" is in the vocabulary. So, we can infer that the model is not perfect, but it is impressive and can be included in your own application.

Running the captioning code on Jupyter for multiple images

Multiple images can also be added as an input string by separating the image path of the different images using commas. The execution time of a string of images will be greater than the times we've seen thus far.

The following is an example of multiple input files:

```
input_files =
'test_images/ballons.jpeg,test_images/bike.jpeg,test_images/dog.jpeg,test_i
mages/fireworks.jpeg,test_images/football.jpeg,test_images/giraffes.jpeg,te
st_images/headphones.jpeg,test_images/laughing.jpeg,test_images/objects.jpe
g,test_images/snowboard.jpeg,test_images/surfing.jpeg'

capts = gen_caption(input_files)
```

We will not be displaying the images, so the output will include only the results. We can see that some of the results are better than others:

```
input_files = 'test_images/ballons.jpeg,test_images/bike.jpeg,test_images/dog.jpeg,test_images/fireworks.jpeg,test_images,

capts = gen_caption(input_files)

Captions for image ballons.jpeg:
  0) a woman standing on a beach flying a kite . (p=0.004793)
  1) a woman is flying a kite on the beach . (p=0.003442)
  2) a young girl flying a kite on a beach . (p=0.002200)
Captions for image bike.jpeg:
  0) a man riding a bike down a dirt road . (p=0.003308)
  1) a man riding a bike down a road . (p=0.002444)
  2) a man riding a bike down a road next to a forest . (p=0.000610)
Captions for image dog.jpeg:
  0) a woman and a dog are on a bench . (p=0.000024)
  1) a woman and a dog are standing on the grass . (p=0.000014)
  2) a woman and a dog are standing on a bench . (p=0.000012)
Captions for image fireworks.jpeg:
  0) a view of a tree in a park . (p=0.000004)
  1) a view of a tree in the middle of a park . (p=0.000003)
  2) a view of a tree in the middle of a city . (p=0.000003)
Captions for image football.jpeg:
  0) a couple of men playing a game of frisbee . (p=0.001167)
  1) a couple of men playing a game of football . (p=0.001053)
  2) a couple of men playing a game of soccer . (p=0.000807)
Captions for image giraffes.jpeg:
  0) a group of giraffe standing next to each other . (p=0.002270)
  1) a group of giraffes are standing in a field (p=0.000959)
  2) a group of giraffe standing next to each other on a field . (p=0.000744)
Captions for image headphones.jpeg:
  0) a woman holding a cell phone in her hand . (p=0.002533)
  1) a woman holding a cell phone up to her ear . (p=0.002143)
  2) a woman holding a cell phone in her hands . (p=0.001198)
Captions for image laughing.jpeg:
  0) a group of people standing next to each other . (p=0.003400)
  1) a man and a woman standing next to each other . (p=0.002685)
  2) a group of people standing in a room . (p=0.001571)
Captions for image objects.jpeg:
  0) a nc of items that are on a table . (p=0.000309)
  1) a nc of items that are sitting on a table . (p=0.000188)
  2) a nc of cellphones that are on a table . (p=0.000186)
Captions for image snowboard.jpeg:
  0) a man flying through the air while riding a snowboard . (p=0.028471)
  1) a man flying through the air while riding skis . (p=0.005110)
  2) a man flying through the air on top of a snowboard . (p=0.001624)
```

This wraps up running the pre-trained image captioning model. We will now cover training our model from scratch and running it on captioned images.

Retraining the captioning model

So, now that we have seen image captioning code in action, we are going to retrain the image captioner on our own desired data. However, we need to know that it will be very time consuming and will need over 100 GB of hard drive space for computations if we want it to process in a reasonable time. Even with a good GPU, it may take a few days or a week to complete the computation. Since we are inclined toward implementing it and have the resources, let's start retraining the model.

In the Notebook, the first step is to download the pre-trained Inception model. The `webbrowser` module will make it easy to open the URL and to download the file:

```
# First download pretrained Inception (v3) model

import webbrowser
webbrowser.open("http://download.tensorflow.org/models/inception_v3_2016_08
_28.tar.gz")

# Completely unzip tar.gz file to get inception_v3.ckpt,
# --recommend storing in im2txt/data directory
```

The following will be the output:

```
In [15]:   # First download pretrained Inception (v3) model

           import webbrowser
           webbrowser.open("http://download.tensorflow.org/models/inception_v3_2016_08_28.tar.gz")

           # Completely unzip tar.gz file to get inception_v3.ckpt,
           # --recommend storing in im2txt/data directory

Out[15]:   True
```

When we select the code block and execute it, we might not be able to view the content on the web page, but we can click **save** on the dialog box to download the file. Unzip the file to get the inception v3 checkpoint file. We can use any of the unzipping utility available, but it is preferable to use 7-zip to get the Inception v3 checkpoint file and store it in `im2txt/data` in the project directory.

The `cd` command is used to navigate to the `im2txt/data` directory, where all our files are present. The `run_build_mscoco_data.py` Python script will grab and process all the image data and the pre-made caption data. This process might take over 100 GB of space and take over an hour to complete its execution.

Once the computation is complete, we will see the three ZIP files in our project's directory. We can unzip these files to get the following directories:

Name	Date modified	Type	Size
annotations	7/22/2018 5:05 AM	File folder	
train2014	8/16/2014 2:08 AM	File folder	
val2014	8/16/2014 1:15 AM	File folder	
captions_train-val2014.zip	7/22/2015 6:55 PM	ZIP File	19,213 KB
train2014.zip	1/16/2016 4:24 PM	ZIP File	13,193,920 KB
val2014.zip	8/15/2014 8:15 PM	ZIP File	6,489,271 KB

The training and validation JSON files are present in the `annotations` folder. The other directories have image training and validation data. Under the `train2014` directory, we will find a bunch of JPEG images corresponding to the training data. Similarly, the resources corresponding to the validation data will be present in the `val2014` folder. We can substitute our own images as well and edit the corresponding JSON file in the `annotations` folder. We will need many examples, as a handful examples will not provide effective results. There are over 80,000 images in the `train2014` directory and processing them will require intensive resources.

Once we execute the `run_build_mscoco_data.py` command, we need to load the required modules:

```
# Now gather and prepare the MSCOCO data

# Comment out cd magic command if already in data directory
%cd im2txt/data
# This command will take an hour or more to run typically.
# Note, you will need a lot of HD space (>100 GB)!
%run build_mscoco_data.py

# At this point you have files in im2txt/data/mscoco/raw-data that you can train
# on, or you can substitute your own data

%cd ..

# load needed modules

import tensorflow as tf

from im2txt import configuration
from im2txt import show_and_tell_model
```

We need to load `configuration` and `show_and_tell_model` in the `im2txt` folder along with TensorFlow. We can run the `cd ..` command to be in the right directory.

Now, we will be defining the following variables:

- `input_file_pattern`: Defines the files pointing to the pre-trained Inception checkpoint, which will be generated from our model
- `train_dir`: Contains the path where the training data was stored after we downloaded and unzipped it
- `train_inception`: Set to `false` since we will not be training our Inception model for the initial run
- `number_of_steps`: One million steps for our function
- `log_every_n_steps`: Set 1 for our function

Here is the code:

```
# Initial training
input_file_pattern = 'im2txt/data/mscoco/train-?????-of-00256'

# change these if you put your stuff somewhere else
inception_checkpoint_file = 'im2txt/data/inception_v3.ckpt'
train_dir = 'im2txt/model'

# Don't train inception for initial run
train_inception = False
number_of_steps = 1000000
log_every_n_steps = 1
```

Now let's define our `train` function. The steps performed in the `train` function are as follows:

1. Create the `train` directory
2. Create the graph file
3. Load the essential files
4. Add the required variables for TensorFlow to start training the model to get the learning rate with the number of batches per epoch delay step
5. Set up the layers
6. Set up the saver for saving and restoring the model checkpoint
7. Call TensorFlow and do the training

The following is our `train` function:

1. Define (but don't run yet) our captioning training function:

```
def train():
    model_config = configuration.ModelConfig()
    model_config.input_file_pattern = input_file_pattern
    model_config.inception_checkpoint_file =
inception_checkpoint_file
    training_config = configuration.TrainingConfig()
```

2. Create the training directory:

```
    train_dir = train_dir
    if not tf.gfile.IsDirectory(train_dir):
        tf.logging.info("Creating training directory: %s",
train_dir)
        tf.gfile.MakeDirs(train_dir)
```

3. Build the TensorFlow graph:

```
    g = tf.Graph()
    with g.as_default():
```

4. Build the model:

```
        model = show_and_tell_model.ShowAndTellModel(
            model_config, mode="train",
train_inception=train_inception)
        model.build()
```

5. Set up the learning rate:

```
        learning_rate_decay_fn = None
        if train_inception:
            learning_rate =
tf.constant(training_config.train_inception_learning_rate)
        else:
            learning_rate =
tf.constant(training_config.initial_learning_rate)
            if training_config.learning_rate_decay_factor > 0:
                num_batches_per_epoch =
(training_config.num_examples_per_epoch /
                                model_config.batch_size)
                decay_steps = int(num_batches_per_epoch *
                        training_config.num_epochs_per_decay)
```

```
              def _learning_rate_decay_fn(learning_rate,
global_step):
                   return tf.train.exponential_decay(
                           learning_rate,
                           global_step,
                           decay_steps=decay_steps,
       decay_rate=training_config.learning_rate_decay_factor,
                           staircase=True)

              learning_rate_decay_fn = _learning_rate_decay_fn
```

6. Set up the training ops:

```
       train_op = tf.contrib.layers.optimize_loss(
                           loss=model.total_loss,
       global_step=model.global_step,
       learning_rate=learning_rate,
       optimizer=training_config.optimizer,
       clip_gradients=training_config.clip_gradients,
       learning_rate_decay_fn=learning_rate_decay_fn)
```

7. Set up the `Saver` for saving and restoring model checkpoints:

```
       saver =
tf.train.Saver(max_to_keep=training_config.max_checkpoints_to_keep)

       # Run training.
       tf.contrib.slim.learning.train(
                           train_op,
                           train_dir,
       log_every_n_steps=log_every_n_steps,
                           graph=g,
                           global_step=model.global_step,
                           number_of_steps=number_of_steps,
                           init_fn=model.init_fn,
                           saver=saver)
```

Hit *Ctrl + Enter* for this code cell, since we can execute this now. After that, we need to call the `train` function:

```
train()
```

This will take a long time to process, even on a good GPU, but if we have the resources and still want to refine the model, run the following code to fine-tuning our `inception` model:

```
# Fine tuning
input_file_pattern = 'im2txt/data/mscoco/train-?????-of-00256'
```

```
# change these if you put your stuff somewhere else
inception_checkpoint_file = 'im2txt/data/inception_v3.ckpt'
train_dir = 'im2txt/model'

# This will refine our results
train_inception = True
number_of_steps = 3000000
log_every_n_steps = 1

# Now run the training (warning: takes even longer than initial
training!!!)
train()
```

The model will run for three million steps. It actually continues from where the initial training completed its process and generate new checkpoints and refined models, before running the `train` function again. This will take even more time to process and provide a good result. We can do this in our Jupyter Notebook by correctly pointing our `checkpoint` path and the path for the vocabulary file:

```
# tell our function where to find the trained model and vocabulary
checkpoint_path = './model'
vocab_file = './model/word_counts.txt'
```

After that, we can rerun code block 4 from the Jupyter Notebook file at `https://github.com/PacktPublishing/Computer-Vision-Projects-with-OpenCV-and-Python-3/blob/master/Chapter01/Section_1-Tensorflow_Image_Captioning.ipynb` to find `gen_caption`.

The last step is to run the following code, as we did before in the *Running the captioning code on Jupyter* section:

```
testfile = 'test_images/ballons.jpeg'

figure()
imshow(imread(testfile))

capts = gen_caption(testfile)
```

Once the computation has been completed, we should get some good results. This wraps up image captioning with TensorFlow.

Summary

In this chapter, we were introduced to different image captioning methods. We learned about the Google Brain im2txt captioning model. While working on the project, we were able to run our pre-trained model on a Jupyter Notebook and analyze the model based on the results. In the last section of the chapter, we retrained our image captioning model from scratch.

In the next chapter, we will cover reading license plates with OpenCV.

Reading License Plates with OpenCV

3

This chapter provides an overview of how to extract and display license plate characters in any sample photo with a license plate in it. OpenCV and its plate utility functions help us find the characters on a license plate, and give us a good taste of how computer vision and image processing work.

In this chapter, we will learn about the following:

- The steps needed to read license plates
- Plate utility functions
- Finding plate characters
- Finding and reading license plates

Identifying the license plate

In this project, we are going to detect and read license plates in photos of cars. We will be performing multiple steps, from locating the license plate to displaying the characters in the located license plate.

Let's refer to the code in Jupyter Notebook needed to analyze our sample images:

```
%pylab notebook
figure()
imshow(imread('tests/p1.jpg'))
```

We get the following photo when we run the code:

We have a photo of a car, with its license plate clearly visible and readable. The challenge is to locate the license plate, isolate it from the rest of the photo, and extract the characters from it.

We can now take a closer look at the license plate using the available utility functions:

There are many algorithms that can help us carry out both these tasks. For example, object detectors such as YOLO: Real-Time Object Detection can do a very good job using the relevant machine learning methods for performing such tasks.

However, we will be looking at a straightforward approach, using conventional image processing and computer vision techniques, instead of complex machine learning techniques such as deep learning and TensorFlow.

The algorithm we will be using will help us learn computer vision and image processing techniques, giving us a better understanding of the project. Let's start with our code and check the plate utility functions we will be using.

Plate utility functions

Let's jump to our code in Jupyter Notebook, in order to understand plate utility functions. We will first embed the imports with our utilities.

We will be importing the following libraries:

- OpenCV (version 3.4)
- NumPy
- Pickle, which lets us save Python data and case functions

Import the libraries as follows:

```
import cv2
import numpy as np
import pickle
def gray_thresh_img(input_image):
    h, w, _ = input_image.shape
    grayimg = cv2.cvtColor(input_image, cv2.COLOR_BGR2HSV)[:,:,2]
    kernel = cv2.getStructuringElement(cv2.MORPH_RECT, (3, 3))
    tophat = cv2.morphologyEx(grayimg, cv2.MORPH_TOPHAT, kernel)
    blackhat = cv2.morphologyEx(grayimg, cv2.MORPH_BLACKHAT, kernel)
    graytop = cv2.add(grayimg, tophat)
    contrastgray = cv2.subtract(graytop, blackhat)
    blurred = cv2.GaussianBlur(contrastgray, (5,5), 0)
    thesholded = cv2.adaptiveThreshold(blurred, 255.0,
    cv2.ADAPTIVE_THRESH_GAUSSIAN_C,
    cv2.THRESH_BINARY_INV, 19, 9)
```

We will be using these libraries to load the k-nearest neighbors classifier for reading characters, which implicitly depends on scikit-learn.

We will now discuss the utilities that will be used in our code.

The gray_thresh_img function and morphological functions

The `gray_thresh_img` function takes an input image and converts it to grayscale. We need the image in grayscale, as color images may cause ambiguity, given that the color of license plates differs depending on the area. The `gray_thres_img` function gives us a binarized image.

We can use morphological operations for pre-processing, as this will help us reduce noise and gaps. This will de-noise our image and remove extraneous features.

Kernels

A kernel is a three-by-three square on which we will be using `tophat`, `blackhat`, and `graytop` operations to create a grayscale image. This will also help us to de-noise the image—noise is usually present in natural images, and is not preferable for computer vision. The image can also be de-noised using Gaussian blur.

We will use adaptive thresholding, which looks at local statistics and averages in an image to check whether it is bright or dim relative to its neighborhood. This is preferred over hard thresholding, as it will binarize our images in a better way.

We use the `return` function to get the gray image and binarized image, as follows:

```
return grayimg, thesholded
```

The matching character function

Let's look at our next function to get the matching characters:

```
def getmatchingchars(char_cands):
    char_list = []
    for char_cand in char_cands:
        ch_matches = [] \n",
        for matching_candidate in char_cands:
            if matching_candidate == char_cand:
                continue
            chardistance = np.sqrt((abs(char_cand.x_cent   -
matching_candidate.x_cent) ** 2) +
            (abs(char_cand.y_cent - matching_candidate.y_cent)**2))
            x = float(abs(char_cand.x_cent - matching_candidate.x_cent))
            y = float(abs(char_cand.y_cent - matching_candidate.y_cent))
```

```
        angle = np.rad2deg(np.arctan(y/x) if x != 0.0 else np.pi/2)
        deltaarea = float(abs(matching_candidate.rect_area -
char_cand.rect_area))\
            / float(char_cand.rect_area)
        deltawidth = float(abs(matching_candidate.rect_w-
char_cand.rect_w))\
            / float(char_cand.rect_w)
        deltaheight = float(abs(matching_candidate.rect_h-
char_cand.rect_h))
            / float(char_cand.rect_h)
        if (chardistance < (char_cand.hypotenuse * 5.0) and
            angle < 12.0 and deltaarea < 0.5 and deltawidth < 0.8
            and deltaheight < 0.2):
            ch_matches.append(matching_candidate)
    ch_matches.append(char_cand)
    if len(ch_matches) < 3:
        continue
    char_list.append(ch_matches)
```

The `getmatchingchars` function helps us find our character candidate based on the
following criteria:

- Size
- Relative distance
- Angle
- Area

If the potential character is a reasonable distance from its neighbors, the angle is not too
large compared to the JSON characters, and the area is not too big, we say that the possible
character is a *character candidate*.

The following code will return a list of characters that are part of a license plate, and then
create a container class that will contain objects such as the width, height, center, diagonal
distance or hypotenuse, and aspect ratio of the character sub-images within our complete
image:

```
    for charlist in getmatchingchars(list(set(char_cands)-
set(ch_matches))):
        char_list.append(charlist)
    break
 return char_list
# information container for possible characters in images
class charclass:
    def __init__(self, _contour):
        self.contour = _contour
        self.boundingRect = cv2.boundingRect(self.contour)
```

```
        self.rect_x, self.rect_y, self.rect_w, self.rect_h =
self.boundingRect
        self.rect_area = self.rect_w * self.rect_h
        self.x_cent = (self.rect_x + self.rect_x + self.rect_w) / 2
        self.y_cent = (self.rect_y + self.rect_y + self.rect_h) / 2
        self.hypotenuse = np.sqrt((self.rect_w ** 2) + (self.rect_h ** 2))
        self.aspect_ratio = float(self.rect_w) / float(self.rect_h)
```

The k-nearest neighbors digit classifier

The pre-trained scikit-learn **k-nearest neighbors** (**k-nn**) digit classifier also needs to be loaded, as follows:

```
# load pre-trained scikit-learn knn digit classifier
    with open('knn.p', 'rb') as f:
      knn = pickle.load(f) "
```

The k-nn classifier compares a small image to a series of images already known to it, to find the closest match.

We are not using complex algorithms for this, because characters in a license plate are similar. This is why we can use the k-nn method, which will make a pixel-by-pixel comparison to find the closest match. The characters on a license plate are not handwritten digits where the font might differ, which would need more computation.

In the classifier, p stands for Pickle, which is how Python stores data.

Finding plate characters

Next, we carry out our initial search to find plate characters. First, we find characters roughly, and then find candidates based on specific criteria.

Let's start with the following line in our Notebook:

```
%pylab notebook
```

We can now execute our function cell for imports, utilities, and to load our libraries:

```
import cv2
import numpy as np
import pickle
def getmatchingchars(char_cands):
    char_list = []
    for char_cand in char_cands:
```

```
            ch_matches = [] \n",
            for matching_candidate in char_cands:
                if matching_candidate == char_cand:
                    continue
                chardistance = np.sqrt((abs(char_cand.x_cent  -
matching_candidate.x_cent) ** 2) +
                    (abs(char_cand.y_cent - matching_candidate.y_cent)**2))
                    x = float(abs(char_cand.x_cent - matching_candidate.x_cent))
                    y = float(abs(char_cand.y_cent - matching_candidate.y_cent))
                    angle = np.rad2deg(np.arctan(y/x) if x != 0.0 else np.pi/2)
                    deltaarea = float(abs(matching_candidate.rect_area -
char_cand.rect_area))\
                    / float(char_cand.rect_area)
                    deltawidth = float(abs(matching_candidate.rect_w-
char_cand.rect_w))\
                    / float(char_cand.rect_w)
                    deltaheight = float(abs(matching_candidate.rect_h-
char_cand.rect_h))
                    / float(char_cand.rect_h)
                if (chardistance < (char_cand.hypotenuse * 5.0) and
                    angle < 12.0 and deltaarea < 0.5 and deltawidth < 0.8
                    and deltaheight < 0.2):
                    ch_matches.append(matching_candidate)
        ch_matches.append(char_cand)
        if len(ch_matches) < 3:
            continue
        char_list.append(ch_matches)

        for charlist in getmatchingchars(list(set(char_cands)-
set(ch_matches))):
            char_list.append(charlist)
        break
    return char_list
# information container for possible characters in images
class charclass:
        def __init__(self, _contour):
            self.contour = _contour
            self.boundingRect = cv2.boundingRect(self.contour)
            self.rect_x, self.rect_y, self.rect_w, self.rect_h =
self.boundingRect
            self.rect_area = self.rect_w * self.rect_h
            self.x_cent = (self.rect_x + self.rect_x + self.rect_w) / 2
            self.y_cent = (self.rect_y + self.rect_y + self.rect_h) / 2
            self.hypotenuse = np.sqrt((self.rect_w ** 2) + (self.rect_h ** 2))
            self.aspect_ratio = float(self.rect_w) / float(self.rect_h)
```

We can now load our input image, which will be used for analysis. We use the `plt` function here instead of OpenCV, as OpenCV by default loads images in **blue green red** (**BGR**) format rather than **red green blue** (**RGB**) format. This is important for your custom projects, but it does not matter for our project since we will be converting the image to grayscale.

Let's load our image:

```
input_image = plt.imread('tests/p5.jpg') #use cv2.imread or
 #import matplotlib.pyplot as plt
 #if running outside notebook
figure()
imshow(input_image)
```

This is the output photo:

Let's take a closer look at the license plate of this car:

We will find the characters from this image. However, we first need to remove the background, which is not important for us. Here, we need to carry out initial pre-processing on the image, using the `gray_thresh_img`, `blurred`, and `morphology` functions, which will help us get rid of the background.

Here is the code for the initial pre-processing:

```
def gray_thresh_img(input_image):
    h, w, _ = input_image.shape
    grayimg = cv2.cvtColor(input_image, cv2.COLOR_BGR2HSV)[:,:,2]
    kernel = cv2.getStructuringElement(cv2.MORPH_RECT, (3, 3))
    tophat = cv2.morphologyEx(grayimg, cv2.MORPH_TOPHAT, kernel)
    blackhat = cv2.morphologyEx(grayimg, cv2.MORPH_BLACKHAT, kernel)
    graytop = cv2.add(grayimg, tophat)
    contrastgray = cv2.subtract(graytop, blackhat)
    blurred = cv2.GaussianBlur(contrastgray, (5,5), 0)
    thesholded = cv2.adaptiveThreshold(blurred, 255.0,
    cv2.ADAPTIVE_THRESH_GAUSSIAN_C,
    cv2.THRESH_BINARY_INV, 19, 9)
```

Let's look at our main code:

```
h, w = input_image.shape[:2]
# We don't use color information
# + we need to binarize (theshold) image to find characters
grayimg, thesholded = gray_thresh_img(input_image)
contours = cv2.findContours(thesholded, cv2.RETR_LIST,
```

```
cv2.CHAIN_APPROX_SIMPLE)[1]
# initialize variables for possible characters/plates in image
char_cands = []
plate_candidates = []
```

We will give the image shape, which is going to return the height, width, and RGB depth of the photo. We don't need RGB depth right now, so we will extract only 2 elements; height and width. Since we will be working on grayscale images and not colored ones, we'll call our handy `gray_thresh_img` function, which will return the gray and binarized thresholded image.

To find the contours, we need sub-images within the image that correspond to the character and then correspond to contours. We will use the `findContours` built-in algorithm from OpenCV to find details of complex shapes such as contours that could possibly be characters and work as our k-nn. We will then initialize our `char_cands` and `plate_candidates` variables.

Let's take our first pass at finding the characters:

```
for index in range(0, len(contours)):
    char_cand = charclass(contours[index])
    if (char_cand.rect_area > 80 and char_cand.rect_w > 2
        and char_cand.rect_h > 8 and 0.25 < char_cand.aspect_ratio
        and char_cand.aspect_ratio < 1.0):
        char_cands.append(char_cand)
```

We will be using the characters to find the license plate, which is a different approach to other machine learning algorithms. This approach will help us understand the process of finding characters better.

We will iterate over all the contours and use the `charclass` class (which we have already defined). This automatically extracts centers, diagonal length, and aspect ratio to determine whether the image is too big or too small, or if the aspect ratio is too skewed From this, we can infer that the character is not a letter or number that will be on the license plate. This helps us consider only contours that meet the geometric criteria.

Finding matches and groups of characters

Once the first pass is done, we will refine our matches to find a group of characters that potentially could belong to a license plate. Refer to the following code:

```
for ch_matches in getmatchingchars(char_cands):
    class blank: pass
    plate_candidate = blank()
```

```
    ch_matches.sort(key = lambda ch: ch.x_cent)
    plate_w = int((ch_matches[len(ch_matches) - 1].rect_x + \
                  ch_matches[len(ch_matches) - 1].rect_w -
ch_matches[0].rect_x) * 1.3)
    sum_char_h = 0
    for ch in ch_matches:
        sum_char_h += ch.rect_h
    avg_char_h = sum_char_h / len(ch_matches)
    plate_h = int(avg_char_h * 1.5)
    y = ch_matches[len(ch_matches) - 1].y_cent - ch_matches[0].y_cen
    r = np.sqrt((abs(ch_matches[0].x_cent
                - ch_matches[len(ch_matches) - 1].x_cent) ** 2)
            + (abs(ch_matches[0].y_cent
                - ch_matches[len(ch_matches) - 1].y_cent) ** 2))
    rotate_angle = np.rad2deg(np.arcsin(y / r))
```

We will iterate over all the potential characters by calling the `getmatchingchars` function we used before, which provides additional filtering based on the criteria. It depends on the angles, trigonometry, width, and height compared to neighboring characters, and also on the kind of neighbors. These criteria help us achieve uniformity.

Once we have our plate candidates, we can create a `blank` object. So, we have a `blank` object with no attributes and create a list of them. We first sort from the center of those characters, which will help us sort from leftmost to rightmost going through the matches.

The `sum_char_h` summation will help us find the average height and width of the characters.

Let's look at the following code:

```
    platex = (ch_matches[0].x_cent + ch_matches[len(ch_matches) -
1].x_cent) / 2
    platey = (ch_matches[0].y_cent + ch_matches[len(ch_matches) -
1].y_cent) / 2
    plate_cent = platex, platey
```

The ideal position of the license plate is perpendicular to the camera. If the license plate is at an angle greater than a particular acceptable angle, or upside down, there is a possibility that we will not be able to read the license plate.

We find our x and y from the code, and correct the angle for the license plate if it is within a reasonable angle.

We then figure out the plate location, and store it for computation later using
`rotationMatrix`. We can do this in one step, based on the angle that we found here. We
want to rotate it about the center of the plate, as follows:

```
    plate_candidate.plateloc = (tuple(plate_cent), (plate_w, plate_h),
rotate_angle)
    rotationMatrix = cv2.getRotationMatrix2D(tuple(plate_cent),
rotate_angle, 1.0)
```

We create our rotated image here, and the `cv2.wrapAffine` function will help us with
stretching, skewing, rotating, and translation, as well as higher-order transformations such
as scaling, stretching, and rotating:

```
    rotated = cv2.warpAffine(input_image, rotationMatrix,
tuple(np.flipud(input_image.shape[:2])))

    plate_candidate.plate_im = cv2.getRectSubPix(rotated, (plate_w,
plate_h), tuple(plate_cent))
    if plate_candidate.plate_im is not None:
        plate_candidates.append(plate_candidate)
```

Once we have our sub-image, which is rotated and centered around plate candidates, we
save it to our plate candidates list, which we initiated earlier. We now have our characters
and our initial guess for our plate candidates, using which we are ready to find and read
our license plate candidates.

Finding and reading license plates with OpenCV

We have already found our characters, which are license plate candidates. Now we need to
determine which characters match, so that we can extract the text data and map the
characters within the license plates.

First, we run each plate candidate through our `gray_thresh_img` function, which does
our de-noising and binarization. In this case, we get a cleaner output because we are using
a sub-image and not the complete image.

This is the extraction code we will use:

```
for plate_candidate in plate_candidates:
    plate_candidate.grayimg, plate_candidate.thesholded = \
                        gray_thresh_img(plate_candidate.plate_im)
    plate_candidate.thesholded = cv2.resize(plate_candidate.thesholded,
                        (0, 0), fx = 1.6, fy = 1.6)
    thresholdValue, plate_candidate.thesholded = \
                        cv2.threshold(plate_candidate.thesholded,
                        0.0, 255.0,
                        cv2.THRESH_BINARY |
cv2.THRESH_OTSU)
```

We will need our characters to be of the same size, since we will be using the k-nn approach, which is case-sensitive. If the size differs, we will receive garbage values. After we have the images sized, we need to perform thresholding, for which we will use the OTSU method.

We then need to find contours within our sub-image, and do a sanity check to make sure that the contours we found within our sub-image meet certain criteria where the size and aspect ratio are reasonable, as follows:

```
contours = cv2.findContours(plate_candidate.thesholded, cv2.RETR_LIST,
    cv2.CHAIN_APPROX_SIMPLE)[1]
plate_chars = []
  for contour in contours:
  char_cand = charclass(contour)
  if (char_cand.rect_area > 80 and char_cand.rect_w > 2
  and char_cand.rect_h > 8 and 0.25 < char_cand.aspect_ratio
  and char_cand.aspect_ratio < 1.0):
  plate_chars.append(char_cand)
```

If the contours do not meet the criteria, it means that we are either not looking at a license plate or not getting good characters.

Once the sanity check is complete, we run our getmatchingchars function, which will ensure we get a good group of characters that are roughly of the same size:

```
plate_chars = getmatchingchars(plate_chars)
    if (len(plate_chars) == 0):
    plate_candidate.chars = \"
    continue
for index in range(0, len(plate_chars)):
    plate_chars[index].sort(key = lambda ch: ch.x_cent)
    filt_matching_chars = list(plate_chars[index])
```

This is a redundancy check, but is necessary for achieving clean and reliable results. We iterate over all the characters from left to right, in order, to check that the characters are sufficiently far apart. We do this because, conceivably, near contours that overlap each other could be characters that overlap, which would never happen in a real license plate.

We need to make sure that the characters are far apart, as we're not detecting the same thing over and over again; we are doing multiple `for` loops here and comparing characters to each other as follows:

```
    for thischar in plate_chars[index]:
for alt_char in plate_chars[index]:
if thischar != alt_char:
chardistance = np.sqrt((abs(thischar.x_cent-alt_char.x_cent)**2)
+ (abs(thischar.y_cent-alt_char.y_cent) ** 2))
if chardistance < (thischar.hypotenuse * 0.3):
if thischar.rect_area < alt_char.rect_area:
if thischar in filt_matching_chars:
filt_matching_chars.remove(thischar)
else:
if alt_char in filt_matching_chars:
filt_matching_chars.remove(alt_char)
```

We need to make sure that everything is centered within our region of interest, so that characters are not lost when we perform actions such as scaling, rotation, and translation while we find our k-nn.

In this code, we go through each character in our character list and each thresholded region, to make sure we resize the region to 20 by 30, which matches our k-nn prediction:

```
    charlistlen = 0
char_index = 0

for index in range(0, len(plate_chars)):
if len(plate_chars[index]) > charlistlen:
charlistlen = len(plate_chars[index])
char_index = index

full_char_list = plate_chars[char_index]
full_char_list.sort(key = lambda ch: ch.x_cent)

plate_candidate.chars = \
for thischar in full_char_list:
roi = plate_candidate.thesholded[thischar.rect_y :
thischar.rect_y + thischar.rect_h,
thischar.rect_x :
thischar.rect_x + thischar.rect_w]
```

```
resized_roi = np.float32(cv2.resize(roi, (20, 30)).reshape((1, -1)))
plate_candidate.chars += str(chr(int(knn.predict(resized_roi)[0])))
```

Now, all these regions are of length 600. NumPy's `reshape` function will map the region by some dimensions for a two-dimensional input, to get 1/600.

The `thischar` function is actually an empty string at the start, but will keep getting populated as we find our k-nn.

Also, we need to make sure that our `plate_candidates` are not blank, while we find our best candidate:

```
if len(plate_candidates) > 0:
    plate_candidates.sort(key = lambda plate_candidate:
                          len(plate_candidate.chars), reverse = True)
    best_plate = plate_candidates[0]
    print("License plate read: " + best_plate.chars + "\n")
```

You may find multiple plate candidates for a given image, but often they're the same thing. You might have just found something with four characters, when there are actually six, or something like that. The one that has the most characters is probably right, but you can take a look at the other candidates as well.

We'll extract and sort by the length of the string again, find the `best_plate`, and print out the results.

Result analysis

When we run our code using the best candidate code block, we get the following result:

```
if len(plate_candidates) > 0:
    plate_candidates.sort(key = lambda plate_candidate:
                          len(plate_candidate.chars), reverse = True)
    best_plate = plate_candidates[0]
    print("License plate read: " + best_plate.chars + "\n")

License plate read: LTLDBENZ
```

Once we get our output, we can display our result using the following code:

```
figure()
imshow(best_plate.thesholded)
```

The displayed image will be as follows:

Although there is an extra character, we can see that our displayed image is very close to the plate characters. We can, check it with our other possible plate characters to get the closest result.

Let's try one more license plate, to check how our code works:

```
input_image = plt.imread('tests/p2.jpg')  #use cv2.imread or
                                           #import matplotlib.pyplot as plt
                                           #if running outside notebook
figure()
imshow(input_image)
```

And here's the output:

```
License plate read: M725M
```

The photo displayed is as follows:

If you just want the sub-image of the plate, you can get it using the following code:

```
imshow(best_plate.plate_im)
```

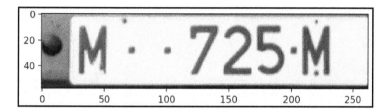

We can find the location of the result as well:

```
figure()
# best_plate.plate_im
imshow(best_plate.plate_im)
best_plate.plateloc
```

You get the following location in the output:

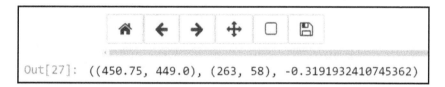

So, here we have the x and y coordinates, width, height, and some offset information.

We can try other available functions, such as the following:

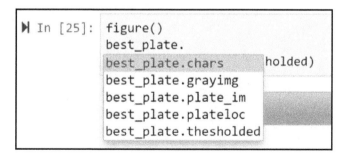

Let's look at another example where the license plate is not clearly visible:

```
input_image = plt.imread('tests/p3.jpg')  #use cv2.imread or
                                          #import matplotlib.pyplot as plt
                                          #if running outside notebook
figure()
imshow(input_image)
```

This gives us the following output:

Let's take a closer look at the license plate:

Our `display` function gives us a pretty good result, as follows:

Let's look at our final example:

```
input_image = plt.imread('tests/p1.jpg')  #use cv2.imread or
                                           #import matplotlib.pyplot as plt
                                           #if running outside notebook

figure()
imshow(input_image)
```

Here's the view:

The following screenshot shows the output:

```
License plate read: HHF9669
```

And the resulting photo is displayed as follows:

Summary

In this chapter, we learned how to perform license plate recognition using OpenCV, giving us a good taste of how computer vision and image processing work.

We first learned the different plate utility functions, which helped us find our plate characters. We then found possible candidates for our license plate characters using OpenCV. Finally, we analyzed our results to check the efficiency of our algorithm.

In the next chapter, Chapter 4, *Human Pose Estimation with TensorFlow*, we're going to use the DeeperCut algorithm, and ArtTrack models for human pose estimation.

Human Pose Estimation with TensorFlow

4

In this chapter, we're going to cover human pose estimation with TensorFlow using the DeeperCut algorithm. We will learn single-person and multi-person pose detection using the DeeperCut and ArtTrack models. Later, we will also learn how to use the model with videos and retrain it to use it for the customized images in our projects.

In this chapter, we will cover the following topics:

- Pose estimation with DeeperCut and ArtTrack
- Single-person pose detection
- Multi-person pose detection
- Videos and retraining

Pose estimation using DeeperCut and ArtTrack

Human pose estimation is the process of estimating the configuration of the body (pose) from an image or video. It includes landmarks (points), which are similar to joints such as the feet, ankles, chin, shoulder, elbows, hands, head, and so on. We will be doing this automatically using deep learning. If you consider a face, the landmarks are relatively rigid or, rather, relatively constant from face to face, such as the relative position of the eyes to the nose, the mouth to the chin, and so forth.

The following photo provides an example:

Although the body structure remains the same, our bodies aren't rigid. So, we need to detect the different parts of our body relative to the other parts. For example, detecting the feet relative to the knee is very challenging compared to facial detection. Also, we can move our hands and feet, which can lead to a wide variety of positions. The following picture gives an example:

This was very difficult until we had some breakthroughs in computer vision from different groups around the world. Different code has been developed to carry out pose estimation, but we will cover an algorithm called **DeeperCut**.

You can refer to MPII Human Pose Models (`pose.mpi-inf.mpg.de`) for detailed information.

DeeperCut was developed by a group in Germany at the Max Planck Society, in conjunction with Stanford University, who released their algorithm and published papers. It is recommended to checkout their paper *DeepCut: Joint Subset Partition and Labeling for Multi Person Pose Estimation*, which gives an overview of an earlier algorithm, before DeeperCut, where they talk about how they detected body parts and how they ran an optimization algorithm to achieve good results. You can also refer to their subsequent paper, *DeeperCuts: a deeper, stronger and faster multi person pose estimation model*, which was published by the same group of authors, as this will cover a lot of the technical details. We will definitely not get exact results, but you can determine things with a reasonable amount of probability.

On the GitHub page, `https://github.com/eldar/pose-tensorflow`, there is the public implementation of their code, which covers DeeperCut and a new version called ArtTrack. It is articulated multi-person tracking in the wild, and you can see the output result in the following photo:

We are going to run a modified version of the code, which is made to run in the Jupyter Notebook environment and is made for all learning purposes, so it should be a little easier than just getting it straight from GitHub. We will learn exactly how we can run the code and use it in our own projects. All of the pre-trained models are included here: `https://github.com/eldar/pose-tensorflow`.

Single-person pose detection

Now that we have an overview of human pose estimation and the new DeeperCut algorithm, we can run the code for single-person pose detection and check that out in the Jupyter Notebook.

We will start with single-person detection. Before starting, we need to make sure that we are using a clean kernel. You can restart your kernel, or you can use the hotkeys to do the same. You can then press the *0* key twice when you're in command mode, which is opposed to edit mode when you're actually editing the cells.

Let's start with our single-person detection code, as shown in the following example:

```
!pip install pyyaml easydict munkres
```

The exclamation mark means execute a shell command. This will install a couple of libraries that you might not have, and if you have Python 3 installed in your system, you might need to change the command to `pip 3`.

In the next cell, we will call the `%pylab notebook` function, which will allow us to look at images with some useful widgets in the notebook, as well as load some numerical libraries, such as `numpy` and so forth. We will do some general imports, such as `os`, `sys` and `cv2`. To do some annotations, we will use `imageio` for the `imread` function and get everything from `randint`. You don't need to import `numpy` because we have already used `%pylab notebook`, but in case you want to copy and paste this code outside of the notebook, you will need it. Then, we need to import `tensorflow`, which already has some glued utilities here that come from the `pose-tensorflow` repository. The code, for your reference, is shown in the following example:

```
%pylab notebook
import os
import sys
import cv2
from imageio import imread
from random import randint
import numpy as np
import tensorflow as tf
from config import load_config
from nnet.net factory import pose_net
```

We then execute the preceding cell.

We will now set up pose prediction, as shown in the following code:

```
def setup_pose_prediction(cfg):
    inputs = tf.placeholder(tf.float32, shape=[cfg.batch_size, None, None,
3])

    outputs = pose_net(cfg).test(inputs)

    restorer = tf.train.Saver()

    sess = tf.Session()

    sess.run(tf.global_variables_initializer())
    sess.run(tf.local_variables_initializer())

    # Restore variables from disk.
    restorer.restore(sess, cfg.init_weights)

    return sess, inputs, outputs
```

It will start our session and load our model. We will be using a pre-trained model, which you can quickly access from the GitHub repository. The `tf.Session()` will start the TensorFlow session and save it to the `sess` variable, which we're going to return. Note that when you run this function, it's going to leave the TensorFlow session open, so if you want to move on and do something else, such as load a new model, then you will have to close the session or restart. It's useful here because we're going to be looking at multiple images and it will be slower if you load the session every single time. We will then take the configuration, which loads the corresponding model and variables, and is going to return the necessary values in order to actually run the model.

Then, we extract CNN outputs using the `extract_cnn_outputs` function. In the output, we'll get joint locations to know where everything is, exactly relative to something else. We want a nice ordered 2D array where we know the X and Y locations of where the ankles, hands, or shoulders are present. This is demonstrated in the following example:

```
def extract_cnn_output(outputs_np, cfg, pairwise_stats = None):
    scmap = outputs_np['part_prob']
    scmap = np.squeeze(scmap)
    locref = None
    pairwise_diff = None
    if cfg.location_refinement:
        locref = np.squeeze(outputs_np['locref'])
        shape = locref.shape
        locref = np.reshape(locref, (shape[0], shape[1], -1, 2))
        locref *= cfg.locref_stdev
    if cfg.pairwise_predict:
```

```
        pairwise_diff = np.squeeze(outputs_np['pairwise_pred'])
        shape = pairwise_diff.shape
        pairwise_diff = np.reshape(pairwise_diff, (shape[0], shape[1], -1,
2))
        num_joints = cfg.num_joints
        for pair in pairwise_stats:
            pair_id = (num_joints - 1) * pair[0] + pair[1] - int(pair[0] <
pair[1])
            pairwise_diff[:, :, pair_id, 0] *=
pairwise_stats[pair]["std"][0]
            pairwise_diff[:, :, pair_id, 0] +=
pairwise_stats[pair]["mean"][0]
            pairwise_diff[:, :, pair_id, 1] *=
pairwise_stats[pair]["std"][1]
            pairwise_diff[:, :, pair_id, 1] +=
pairwise_stats[pair]["mean"][1]
    return scmap, locref, pairwise_diff
```

This is going to take the output from the neural network (which is kind of unintelligible) and put it in a form we can actually use. Then, we will feed the output to something else, or just visualize it in this case. `argmax_pose_predict` is complementary to what we did before. It is another utility function that is going to help us understand the output, which is shown in the following example:

```
def argmax_pose_predict(scmap, offmat, stride):
    """Combine scoremat and offsets to the final pose."""
    num_joints = scmap.shape[2]
    pose = []
    for joint_idx in range(num_joints):
        maxloc = np.unravel_index(np.argmax(scmap[:, :, joint_idx]),
                                  scmap[:, :, joint_idx].shape)
        offset = np.array(offmat[maxloc][joint_idx])[::-1] if offmat is not
None else 0
        pos_f8 = (np.array(maxloc).astype('float') * stride + 0.5 * stride
+
                  offset)
        pose.append(np.hstack((pos_f8[::-1],
                               [scmap[maxloc][joint_idx]])))
    return np.array(pose)
```

Let's now execute that cell in which we have defined the functions. It will run instantly.

The following code will load the configuration file, which is `demo/pose_cfg.yaml`, and `setup_pose_prediction(cfg)` will return `sess`, `inputs`, and `outputs`. This is shown in the following example:

```
cfg = load_config("demo/pose_cfg.yaml")
```

```
sess, inputs, outputs = setup_pose_prediction(cfg)
```

When we run the preceding code, it will leave the TensorFlow session open and it is recommended to run it only once to avoid errors, or you might have to restart the kernel. So, if the command gets executed, we understand that the model has been loaded, as you can see in the following output:

```
INFO:tensorflow:restoring parameters from models/mpii/mpii-single-
resnet-101
```

Now, we'll see how to actually apply the model:

```
file_name = "testcases/standing-lef-lift.jpg"
image = np.array(imread(file_name))
image_batch = np.expand_dims(image, axis=0).astype(float)
outputs_np = sess.run(outputs, feed_dict={inputs: image_batch})
scmap, locref, pairwise_diff = extract_cnn_output(outputs_np, cfg)
pose = argmax_pose_predict(scmap, locref, cfg.stride)
```

For our model, we have to give our file a name. So, we have a directory called `testcases` with a bunch of stock photos of people in various poses, which we will be using for our test. We then need to load the `standing-leg-lift.jpg` image in a suitable format. We will convert the image to something that TensorFlow actually needs. The input is like an `image_batch`, which is going to expand the dimensions along the 0 axis. So, just create an array that TensorFlow can actually use. Then, `outputs_np` will run the session, extract the CNN output in the next line, and then do the actual pose prediction. The `pose` variable is the best to use here. We should then execute the cell and hit *Esc* button to get into the command mode. Then, we need to create a new cell; type `pose` and hit *Ctrl* + *Enter*. We will then get the following 2D array output:

```
array([[154.21713603, 369.49524975,  0.97495675],
       [144.66004324, 280.38701272,  0.97836888],
       [130.74821067, 181.00517952,  0.89270324],
       [174.04091334, 171.14334095,  0.88625103],
       [235.90207493, 241.08008146,  0.97764331],
       [301.39780343, 302.21447849,  0.92958534],
       [ 99.43290633, 168.43356824,  0.98397946],
       [ 63.96742463, 127.38911414,  0.99213421],
       [101.82382166,  76.10697242,  0.99111789],
       [180.59155178,  73.29837465,  0.99223047],
       [224.60096455, 109.43770075,  0.99714881],
       [191.66644788, 148.67574054,  0.99290884],
       [139.69199833,  52.24837098,  0.9979133 ],
       [138.82638311,   3.14040202,  0.98071539]])
```

The output gives us the x and y coordinates corresponding to the joints such as wrists, ankles, knees, head, chin, shoulders, and so on. From this, we get the x coordinate, y coordinate, and matching score. We do not need the sub-pixel level, so we can round it to the nearest integer. In the following example, you can see that we have labeled our opposing joints with numbers and drawn lines between them:

```python
pose2D = pose[:, :2]
image_annot = image.copy()

for index in range(5):
    randcolor = tuple([randint(0, 255) for i in range(3)])
    thickness = int(min(image_annot[:,:,0].shape)/250) + 1
    start_pt = tuple(pose2D[index].astype('int'))
    end_pt = tuple(pose2D[index+1].astype('int'))
    image_annot = cv2.line(image_annot, start_pt, end_pt, randcolor,
thickness)
for index in range(6,11): #next bunch are arms/shoulders (from one hand to
other)
    randcolor = tuple([randint(0,255) for i in range(3)])
    thickness = int(min(image_annot[:,:,0].shape)/250) + 1
    start_pt = tuple(pose2D[index].astype('int'))
    end_pt = tuple(pose2D[index+1].astype('int'))
    image_annot = cv2.line(image_annot, start_pt, end_pt, randcolor,
thickness)
#connect Line from chin to top of head
image_annot = cv2.line(image_annot,
                    tuple(pose2D[12].astype('int')),
tuple(pose2D[13].astype('int'))
                    tuple([randint(0,255) for i in range(3)]),
thickness)
```

We need to create a `pose2D` label here, and then we are going to extract the x and y coordinates in the first two columns. We will make a copy using `image.copy()`, because we want our annotated image to be separate from our original image.

We will run the following code to show our original image:

```python
figure()
imshow(image)
```

We are now going to learn how to annotate the original image. We're going to create a copy of the image and then we're going to iterate it over the first six joints and draw lines between them. It starts on the ankle, 1, goes up through the hips, and then goes down to the the other ankle. Numbers 6 through 11 will be the arms and shoulders, and the last two points are the chin and the top of the head. We're now going to connect all these points with lines from our pose2D. We actually don't have points for the waist and the collar, but we can easily estimate those from the midpoints of the hips and the shoulders, which is useful for completing the skeleton.

Let's look at the following code, which helps us estimate the midpoints:

```
# There no actual joints on waist or coLLar,
# but we can estimate them from hip/shoulder midpoints
waist = tuple(((pose2D[2]+pose2D[3])/2).astype('int'))
collar = tuple(((pose2D[8]+pose2D[9])/2).astype('int'))
# draw the "spine"
image_annot = cv2.line(image_annot, waist, collar,
                    tuple([randint(0,255) for i in range(3)]),
thickness)
image_annot = cv2.line(image_annot, tuple(pose2D[12].astype('int')),
collar,
                    tuple([randint(0,255) for i in range(3)]),
thickness)
# now Label the joints with numbers
font = cv2.FONT_HERSHEY_SIMPLEX
fontsize = min(image_annot[:,:,0].shape)/750 #scale the font size to the
image size
for idx, pt in enumerate(pose2D):
    randcolor = tuple([randint(0,255) for i in range(3)])
image_annot = cv2.putText(image_annot, str(idx+1),
                    tuple(pt.astype('int')),font, fontsize,
                    randcolor,2,cv2.LINE_AA)
figure()
imshow(image_annot)
```

We can now draw a spine by drawing a point from the waist to the collar, and the collar to the chin. We can also label these joints to show exactly what we are joining, and this will help in your customized application. We are going to label the joints, create the figure, show the annotated image, and deal with random colors. The following screenshot shows what the output looks like:

Here, **1** is the right ankle, but it could be the left ankle depending on which way the person's facing. So, all the links are joined except for **13**, which is a bit occluded here, and **14**, which is slightly out of the image. The nice thing about this is that it potentially works even if other joints are occluded (for instance, if they're off-screen or covered up by something). You will notice that the image is simple with a flat background, flat floor, and a simple pose and clothes. The code will also work with more complicated images, and if you have any trouble reading the details, you can use the widgets here and zoom in.

Let's try using different images and analyze our results, which are shown in the following example:

```
file_name = "testcases/mountain_pose.jpg"
image = np.array(imread(file_name))
image_batch = np.expand_dims(image, axis=0).astype(float)
outputs_np = sess.run(outputs, feed_dict={inputs: image_batch})
scmap, locref, pairwise_diff = extract_cnn_output(outputs_np, cfg)
pose = argmax_pose_predict(scmap, locref, cfg.stride)
```

The following shows the photo we will be testing:

When we run our model again, using a different image, we get the following output:

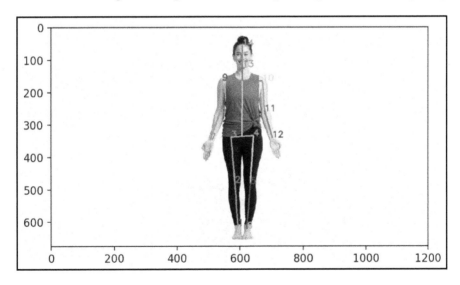

If we take an image of a guy with crossed arms, We get the following screenshot:

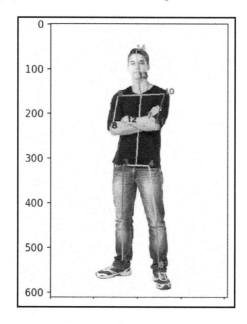

The result is very good, even though the arms are crossed.

Now, let's take a look at a few difficult images. This might not give us the accurate results of a complete motion capture pose estimation solution, but is still very impressive.

Select acrobatic.jpeg, which is as follows:

The output we get when we run this photo is shown in the following example:

It looks as if it found the joints, more or less, but did not connect them properly. It shows that the guy's head is on his hand, which is touching the ground. We can see that the results are not that good. But we cannot expect accurate results for all images, even though this is state of the art.

Multi-person pose detection

Now, let's move from single-person pose detection to multi-person pose detection. With single-person pose detection, we saw that the code will take an image of a single person and generate pose estimation with all the joints labeled. We will now learn a more advanced model called ArtTrack, which will allow us to count the number of people, find people, and estimate their poses.

Let's look at the code for multi-person pose detection, which is shown in the following example:

```
import os
import sys
import numpy as np
import cv2 I
from imageio import imread, imsave
from config import load_config
from dataset.factory import create as create_dataset
```

```
from nnet import predict
from dataset.pose_dataset import data_to_input
from multiperson.detections import extract_detections
from multiperson.predict import SpatialModel, eval_graph,
get_person_conf_multicut
# from muLtiperson.visuaLize import PersonDraw, visuaLize_detections
```

This is a little more complicated. We will first list our directories here using the `!ls` command in the current directory, where you will find a file called `compile.sh`.

We need to run this file because there are some binary dependencies in this module. But this is a shell script file, and you might face some issues on macOS or Linux. So, in order to generate those files/commands that are OS-specific, you will need to run that script. For Windows, those binary files have already been generated. So, if you are using the latest version of Python and TensorFlow, then the files will be compatible and the binary should work.

If it does not work, you will need to download and install Visual Studio Community. There are some instructions that you can follow at `https://github.com/eldar/pose-tensorflow` under the `demo` code section for multi-person pose.

Once you have everything up and running, we can start with our example. Also, as we have already discussed, we need to make sure that we restart the kernel. This is important because if you have your session already open for running a different project, TensorFlow might not be able to compute the code as the previous model is loaded. It is always a good practice to start from a fresh kernel.

We will run our `%pylab notebook` to make our visualizations and numerix. The code works similarly to what we have already covered, where we have the boilerplate and load a pre-trained model. The pre-trained model is already included, so we don't need to download it. The code will execute within a second because of TensorFlow, and we will get the modules imported and load the repositories as well. Also, we need to load the model and actually do the predictions separately. If we hit *Ctrl* + *Shift* + *-*, we can separate the predictions into different cells to make it look neat.

When we run the first cell, we get the following output:

```
Populating the interactive namespace from numpy and matplotlib

C:\Users\mrever\Anaconda3\lib\site-packages\IPython\core\magics\pylab.py:160:
UserWarning: pylab import has clobbered these variables: ['imread', 'imsave']
`%matplotlib` prevents importing * from pylab and numpy
  "\n`%matplotlib` prevents importing * from pylab and numpy"
```

This is not a big error message, and is because `imread` was defined here; the Notebook clobbers that and just gives you a warning message. We can just rerun that code to ignore the warning and get a tidy output.

In this cell, we are going load the configuration file for multiple people provided by the authors of ArtTrack/DeeperCut.

The following line loads the dataset:

```
cf = load_config("demo/pose_cfg_multi.yaml)
```

Then, the following line creates the model and loads it:

```
dataset = create_dataset(cfg)
sm = SpatialModel(cfg)
sm.load()
sess, inputs, outputs = predict.setup_pose_prediction(cfg)
```

When we execute that, we get the following output:

```
INFO:tensorflow:Restoring parameters from models/coco/coco-resnet-101
```

We will keep the session open here so that we can keep running different things and quickly run through different frames.

We will now run our code for some test cases that actually have multiple people, as follows:

```
file_name = "testcases/bus_people.jpg"
image = np.array(imread(file_name))
image_batch = data_to_input(image)
# Compute prediction with the CNN
outputs_np = sess.run(outputs, feed_dict={inputs: image_batch})
scmap, locref, pairwise_diff = predict.extract_cnn_output(outputs_np, cfg,
dataset
detections = extract_detections(cfg, scmap, locref, pairwise_diff)
unLab, pos_array, unary_array, pwidx_array, pw_array = eval_graph(sm,
detections)
person_conf_multi = get_person_conf_multicut(sm, unLab, unary_array,
pos_array)
image_annot = image.copy()
for pose2D in person_conf_multi:
    font = cv2.FONT_HERSHEY_SIMPLEX
    fontsize = min(image_annot[:,:,0].shape)/1000
```

We need to go to the `np.array` and convert it to a flat array network to compute the predictions with `sess.run`, and then extract the CNN output and `detections` using the model utilities. We will not label the bones here, but we will instead label the joints with numbers.

When we run the code, we get the following output:

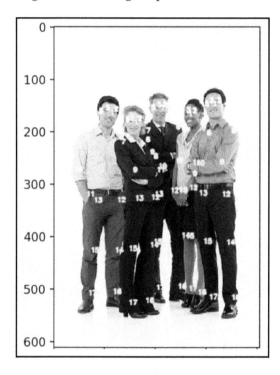

This is a simple image of multiple people, in plain dress and with a flat background. This actually worked. However, the numbers aren't the same as before. Previously, number **1** corresponded to the right ankle and went up through **2**, **3**, **4**, **5**, and **6**, and then **7** was the right wrist, and so on. So, the numbers are different, and there are more of them, which actually detects more joints because they have multiple numbers for the face, so there are multiple points here. Let's zoom in to check the details, as shown in the following picture:

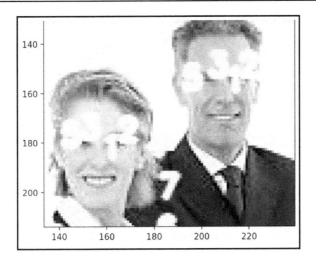

Here, we have the facial landmarks as **1**, **2**, **3**, **4**, and **5**, and hence this could be used in conjunction with the dlib detector, which is covered in Chapter 6, *Facial Feature Tracking and Classification with dlib*. If we want to know somebody's facial expression, in addition to the full-body landmark detectors and their pose, then this could be done here. We can also get a really thorough description of which way people are facing and exactly what they're doing within the image.

Let's try another `exercise_class.jpeg` image, which gives us the following output:

Here, we can see how multiple points are present on the knees for the lady on the extreme right. It is still a good result.

Let's try one more image, which we saw previously on the GitHub page, `gym.png`.

You can see the output as follows:

This does detect the body parts here. So, let's try using this model to detect the pose for a single person. Do you think it will work? The answer is *yes*, it does work. You must be wondering why we would use the previous model if this is available. This model is slightly more computationally efficient, so if you know you only have one person, you don't actually need it, because this algorithm provides the number of people.

You can select the photo of a single person from among the photos available. For example, we'll select `mountain_pose.jpg`, which gives the following output:

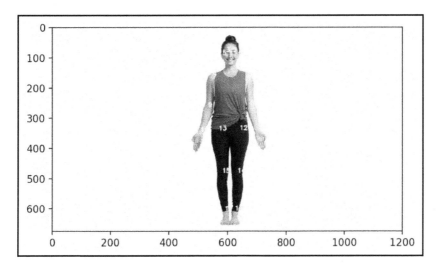

It will also show the number of people, as demonstrated by the following code:

```
num_people:    1
```

But, if you use the multi-person detector for a single person, it might be prone to over-fitting and detecting more people than are actually in the image. So, if you already know there is only one person, then it may still be a good idea to just use that original model rather than the ArtTrack model. But if it does work, try both, or use whatever is best for your application. However, this might not work perfectly for complex images and a complicated variety of poses.

Let's try one last `island_dance.jpeg` image. The following screenshot shows the result:

Retraining the human pose estimation model

We will now discuss how to handle videos and retrain our human pose estimation network. We have already covered face detection and how to apply a model to a video. Opening a video is pretty straightforward and OpenCV provides a mechanism for that. It's basically doing the same thing one frame at a time. The following example shows the code for this:

```
predictor_path = "./shape_predictor_68_face_landmarks.dat"
detector = dlib.get_frontal_face_detector()
predictor = dlib.shape_predictor(predictor_path)

#Uncomment Line below if you want to use your webcam
#cap = cv2.VideoCapture(0) #0 is the first camera on your computer, change
if you
#more than one camera

#Comment out the Line below if using webcam
cap = cv2.VideoCapture('./rollerc.mp4')
figure(100)
font = cv2.FONT_HERSHEY_SIMPLEX
```

First, we need to create a `cv2` capture device, then open the file, and while reading the file, we should load the image and run the network on the image. Please refer to the following code:

```
font = cv2.FONT_HERSHEY_SIMPLEX
while(True):
    #Capture frame-by-frame
    ret, img = cap.read()
    img.flags['WRITEABLE']=True #just in case
    try:
        dets = detector(img, 1)
        shape = predictor(img, dets[0])
    except:
        print('no face detected', end='\r')
        cap.release()
        break
#similar to previous example, except frame-by-frame here
    annotated=img.copy()
    head_width = shape.part(16).x-shape.part(6).x
    fontsize = head_width/650
    for pt in range(68):
        x,y = shape.part(pt).x, shape.part(pt).y
        annotated=cv2.putText(annotated, str(pt), (x,y), font, fontsize,
(255,255,255), 2, cv2.LINE_AA)

#Let's see our results
    fig=imshow(cv2.cvtColor(annotated,cv2.COLOR_BGR2RGB)) #OpenCV uses BGR
format

    display.clear_output(wait=True)
    display.display(gcf())

#When everything is done, release the capture
cap.release()
```

Using a good GPU, we should be able to do the computation in few frames per second, if not 30 to 60 FPS, depending on your hardware. You should be able to do it almost in real time.

For training your model, you need to first make sure that you have good hardware and a lot of time. First, you need to download the ImageNet and ResNet models. Then, you need to go through the steps and instructions on the `https://github.com/eldar/pose-tensorflow/blob/master/models/README.md` page. You will need a lot of data, so you can use the data they provide. Using your own data could be time consuming and difficult to obtain, but it is possible. You can refer to the previous link provided for complete instructions.

The instructions here use MATLAB at one point to convert the data, although there are ways to do that in Python and train the model with the MS COCO dataset. This is similar to what we did in Chapter 2, *Image Captioning with TensorFlow* and it also provides instructions on how to train the model with your own data set. This involves a lot of work and a lot of computational power. You can try this or use what has already been provided in the pre-trained model, which can do a lot of things.

Summary

In this chapter, we learned the basics of human pose estimation and then used the DeeperCut and ArtTrack models in our project for human pose estimation. Using these models, we carried out single-person and multi-person pose detection. Towards the end of the chapter, we learned how to use the model with videos and retrained the model for customized images.

In the next chapter, Chapter 5, *Handwritten Digit Recognition with scikit-learn and TensorFlow*, we will learn handwritten digit recognition with scikit-learn and TensorFlow.

5
Handwritten Digit Recognition with scikit-learn and TensorFlow

In this chapter, we are going to learn how machine learning can be applied to computer vision projects, using a couple of different Python modules. We will also create and train a support vector machine that will actually perform our digit classification.

In this chapter, we will be covering the following topics:

- Acquiring and processing MNIST digit data
- Creating and training a support vector machine
- Applying the support vector machine to new data
- Introducing TensorFlow with digit classification
- Evaluating the results

Acquiring and processing MNIST digit data

As mentioned, we will be covering handwritten digit recognition with scikit-learn and TensorFlow. Here, we're going to learn how machine learning can be applied to computer vision projects, and we're going to learn a couple of different ways and models, using a couple of different Python modules. Let's get started.

You have probably heard about machine learning. Here, we will be particularly talking about supervised machine learning, where we have a bunch of examples that we want to accomplish. So, rather than explicitly telling the computer what we want, we give an example.

Let's take the case of the handwritten digits 0 through 9, which have labels that are created by humans indicating what those digits are supposed to be. So, rather than hand-coding features and explicitly telling the computer what the algorithm is, we are going to construct a model where we take those inputs, optimize some functions like a set of variables, and then train the computer to put the outputs to be what we want them to be.

So, we will go through handwritten digits, starting with 0, 1, 2, 3, and so on. That's the general paradigm of machine learning, and we're going to cover three different algorithms here.

So, let's start running some code.

Open up your Jupyter Notebook and, as we did in the previous chapter, let's start fresh in this chapter. As you can observe in the following code, we will be importing our essential modules, such as numpy, which is the foundation of numerical computing in Python:

```
#import necessary modules here
#--the final notebook will have complete codes that can be
#--copied out into self-contained .py scripts

import numpy as np
import matplotlib.pyplot as plt
import cv2
import sys
import tempfile

from sklearn import svm, metrics
import tensorflow as tf

from tensorflow.examples.tutorials.mnist import input_data
```

As you can see in the preceding code, we are importing pyplot, so that we can visualize what we are doing. We will also use a little bit of OpenCV for converting some images. We will also be using scikit-learn, which is abbreviated as sklearn in the actual module, while importing a support vector machine, as well as some tools that will give us our metrics. This will tell us how well things have actually worked. We will also be importing TensorFlow, with the abbreviation as tf, as we will be obtaining our data from it.

One main advantage of scikit-learn and TensorFlow is that they have built-in functionality for getting digit recognition, which is such a common thing in computer vision and machine learning packages. So, you don't need to go to websites and download it, and then write the lines yourself. It will be taken care of for you. Hence, scikit-learn actually has a good number of inbuilt datasets, some for computer vision, some for other tasks. It has a digit example, and we can then choose which datasets are available from the inbuilt datasets by writing `datasets` and then pressing *Tab*, as shown in the following screenshot:

```
#what kind of data do we already have?
from sklearn import datasets
digits=datasets.load_digits()

datasets.|
example_ base
print(ty california_housing
plt.imsh clear_data_home
example_ covtype
         data
         descr
#acquire dump_svmlight_file
#http:// fetch_20newsgroups
         fetch_20newsgroups_vectorized
data_dir fetch_california_housing
```

Now, we have a list of inbuilt datasets. For example, you want to know `california_housing` prices; that is, you want estimated housing prices based on things like square footage and the number of bedrooms in the house—there's a dataset for that. Some of this is image data, some is not. So, this might be something you want to check out if you want to experiment with different machine learning techniques, but for the `dataset.load_digits()` one, we have the following code that shows what it does:

```
#what kind of data do we already have?
from sklearn import datasets
digits=datasets.load_digits()


example_image=digits.images[0]
print(type(example_image))
plt.imshow(example_image); plt.show()
example_image.reshape((8*8,1))
```

Let's break it down and understand the code. Firstly, we load an example image, just the first image in the set, as follows:

```
example_image=digits.images[0]
print(type(example_image))
```

The data is actually stored in images and it's an array of examples where each one is an 8 x 8 handwritten digit image.

Next, we plot the image as follows:

```
plt.imshow(example_image); plt.show()
example_image.reshape((8*8,1))
```

We should see the following output:

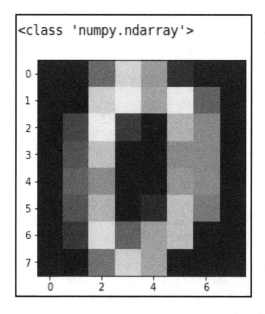

But I like to work with a slightly higher resolution example that we're going to see from MNIST later. The lower resolution images are a little computationally faster to use because they're smaller images. If we want to preprocess these images, these are stored as 8 x 8, and we need to convert each of them to a 1D array. We can do that easily using the reshape function, which we have used in our previous code:

```
example_image.reshape((8*8,1))
```

This will provide us with an output where, instead of an 8 x 8 array, we get a 1 x 64 array, as follows:

```
Out[2]:  array([[  0.],
                 [  0.],
                 [  5.],
                 [ 13.],
                 [  9.],
                 [  1.],
                 [  0.],
                 [  0.],
                 [  0.],
                 [ 13.],
                 [ 15.],
                 [ 10.],
                 [ 15.],
                 [  5.],
                 [  0.],
                 [  0.],
                 [  3.],
                 [ 15.],
                 [  2.],
                 [  0.],
                 [ 11.],
                 [  8.],
                 [  0.],
                 [  0.],
                 [  4.],
                 [ 12.],
```

Now, we are going to use the MNIST data that is available from the following website:

```
http://yann.lecun.com/exdb/mnist/
```

It is a fairly standard dataset. TensorFlow is nice enough to provide some functionality for getting that data, so you don't have to go to the website and manually download it. We need to define `data_dir` and specify a location to save the data to. So, just create this `/tmp/tensorflow/mnist/input_data` directory and this will be fine, regardless of the operating system you're running, and then we have some `input_data` that we imported from `tensorflow` and `read_data_sets`. Now, let's run the following code:

```
#acquire standard MNIST handwritten digit data
#http://yann.lecun.com/exdb/mnist/

data_dir = '/tmp/tensorflow/mnist/input_data'
mnist = input_data.read_data_sets(data_dir, one_hot=True)
```

We should get the following output:

```
#acquire standard MNIST handwritten digit data
#http://yann.lecun.com/exdb/mnist/

data_dir = '/tmp/tensorflow/mnist/input_data'
mnist = input_data.read_data_sets(data_dir, one_hot=True)

Successfully downloaded train-images-idx3-ubyte.gz 9912422 bytes.
Extracting /tmp/tensorflow/mnist/input_data/train-images-idx3-ubyte.gz
Successfully downloaded train-labels-idx1-ubyte.gz 28881 bytes.
Extracting /tmp/tensorflow/mnist/input_data/train-labels-idx1-ubyte.gz
Successfully downloaded t10k-images-idx3-ubyte.gz 1648877 bytes.
Extracting /tmp/tensorflow/mnist/input_data/t10k-images-idx3-ubyte.gz
Successfully downloaded t10k-labels-idx1-ubyte.gz 4542 bytes.
Extracting /tmp/tensorflow/mnist/input_data/t10k-labels-idx1-ubyte.gz
```

If you don't have the files, the code will download the gzip files and, if you do already have them, it just reads the existing gzip files and stores them in the `mnist` variable. `one_hot=True` ensures you get the labels, in terms of vectors, which means instead of being labeled with an American numerals like zero, one, two, three, four, and so on, it's going to be an array of mostly zeros. It's going to be an array of length 10, where everything is 0 except for one thing, which will be 1. So, if we have, for example, 0, 1, 0, 0, 0, 0, and so on, that would represent a 1 and, if it was a 9, it would be all zeros until the last one, which would be a 1. So, it's one useful way for machine learning to label an output. This is the way we got the data and we're going to be using it; it's more helpful for when we actually use TensorFlow, but for scikit-learn it actually does need the numerics.

Let's understand the data before we dive in and do some actual machine learning. We have the `mnist` variable, and it's already separated into training and testing data. With machine learning, you don't want to train on all of your data; you don't want to build your model with all of your data because then you won't know how well it's going to handle new data examples that it hasn't seen before. What you want to do is split it into training data and testing data. So, the training data is going to build a model, and the test data is going to validate it. So, the splitting of the data is already done for us, just with the following variables:

```
#now we load and examine the data
train_data=mnist.train.images
print(train_data.shape)
n_samples = train_data.shape[0]


train_labels=np.array(np.where(mnist.train.labels==1))[1]

plt.imshow(train_data[1000].reshape((28,28))); plt.show()
```

Let's break down the code for better understanding.

Firstly, we load `train_data` from `train.images`, as follows:

```
#now we load and examine the data
train_data=mnist.train.images
```

We're going to see what the shape is to understand it using `.shape`, as follows:

```
print(train_data.shape)
```

If you need to know the number of samples, we can extract that from the `shape` output, as follows:

```
n_samples = train_data.shape[0]
```

Again, it is a NumPy array, so all NumPy functions and features are there.

Then, execute the following code for `train_labels`:

```
train_labels=np.array(np.where(mnist.train.labels==1))[1]
plt.imshow(train_data[1000].reshape((28,28))); plt.show()
```

Here, we just see where the `train.label` equals 1 and we extract that to create an array of those values, which will give us our `train_labels`. So, a 1D array corresponds to the number of examples where it contains the actual output of each one. We'll see just an example; let's take `1000` out of `55000` training examples.

Running this code gives us the following output:

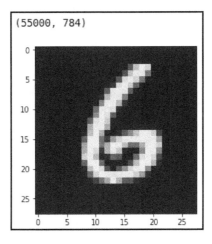

784 is the number of pixels in the image and that's because they are 28 by 28 squares, *28 x 28 = 784*. So, we have, 55000 examples 784 pixels, or we call them features, and then the train_labels is going to be of length 55000 and the other dimension is just 1. Here's an example. This data already comes in a 1D array, so that was why we used the reshape function and passed the 28 by 28 value, in order to convert it to an actual image that we can see.

Great, our data is loaded and processed and is ready to be used, so we can begin actual machine learning. Now that our data is set up and ready to go, we can move on to our next section, in which we will create and train our support vector machine and perform our digit classification.

Creating and training a support vector machine

In this section, we're going to create and train a support vector machine that will actually perform our digit classification.

In the very first example, we're going to use scikit-learn, and we're going to use what's called a support vector machine, which is a very powerful, very versatile classic machine learning technique that can learn all kinds of functions and all kinds of mappings from inputs to outputs. We're going to do classification, which is mapping inputs as an array of pixels, and in our case we're going to classify each input into one of ten classes, corresponding to ten digits. But we can classify different kinds of things as continuous ordered functions, which is called regression, and that can be useful, for example, if you want to extract position or an area of volume where it doesn't just fit into a neat category.

For this section, we're going to be doing primarily classification. So, scikit-learn makes it very easy to create such a model. A support vector classifier can be called with svm.SVC, in which support vector machine came from sklearn package and we have this meta parameter for the model called gamma, just kind of an inverse radius, the area of influence of the sport vectors, as shown in the following code:

```
# Create a classifier: a support vector classifier
classifier = svm.SVC(gamma=0.001)
# Learn about gamma and other SVM parameters here:
# http://scikit-learn.org/stable/auto_examples/svm/plot_rbf_parameters.html
# Exercise: Experiment with the parameters to see how they affect execution
# time and accuracy

# Train the model -- we're only going to use the training data (and not
```

```
# the test data) to ensure that our model generalizes to unseen cases.
# This (training) is typically what takes the most computational time
# when doing machine learning.
classifier.fit(train_data, train_labels)
```

How the support vector machine works is not covered here, as there is plenty of literature available on that subject, and it's not absolutely necessary to understand it fully in order to learn it. Now, we're just going to see how we can apply this for some cases.

The gamma parameter is something I recommend you experiment with as an exercise. We're going to start with a known gamma parameter that will work well for our case, namely .001, but you should learn about the other parameters that are available. I recommend going to http://scikit-learn.org/stable/auto_examples/svm/plot_rbf_parameters. html and again I recommend playing with this to see how it affects execution time and accuracy. But, what's important to take away here is that we can create our model with just one line. It defines the model but we haven't actually trained it. We haven't actually given any data and made it fit its parameters such that it will actually produce a desirable output. Now, if we feed it an image of five, it will say, that's OK, this is a 5. So, in order to do that, we have to fit it.

In the preceding code, we have created our classifier and it's very simple: classifier. fit. We give it the train_data and the train_labels that we got from our previous code execution. Just a heads up, this execution is going to take a few minutes; it generally does. Usually, the training process is the slowest part of machine learning. That's typically the case but this shouldn't be too bad. This only takes a couple of minutes and, again, we're just using your training data so that we can verify that this will generalize to unseen cases.

Now that we've seen our support vector machine and it's actually been trained, we can move on to our next section, where we apply the support vector machine to new data that it was not trained upon.

Applying the support vector machine to new data

Now that we have our trained support vector machine, we can actually apply the support vector machine to new data that hasn't been seen and see that our digit classifier is actually working.

After the cell has executed successfully and if everything worked correctly, we should see the following output:

```
# Create a classifier: a support vector classifier
classifier = svm.SVC(gamma=0.001)
# Learn about gamma and other SVM parameters here:
# http://scikit-learn.org/stable/auto_examples/svm/plot_rbf_parameters.html
# Exercise:  Experiment with the parameters to see how they affect execution
#            time and accuracy

# Train the model -- we're only going to use the training data (and not
# the test data) to ensure that our model generalizes to unseen cases.
# This (training) is typically what takes the most computational time
# when doing machine learning.
classifier.fit(train_data, train_labels)

SVC(C=1.0, cache_size=200, class_weight=None, coef0=0.0,
  decision_function_shape='ovr', degree=3, gamma=0.001, kernel='rbf',
  max_iter=-1, probability=False, random_state=None, shrinking=True,
  tol=0.001, verbose=False)
```

This is just the output from creating the support vector classifier. This just gives information about the metadata parameters that we used; we used what's known as a radial basis function kernel, and fitting the data did not produce any error messages. So, that means the code has worked. So, now we have our trained model, we want to see how well it's going to work on data that it hasn't seen.

Now, we're going to get our test data, as follows:

```
# Now predict the value of the digit on the test data:
test_data=mnist.test.images
test_labels=np.array(np.where(mnist.test.labels==1))[1]

expected = test_labels
predicted = classifier.predict(test_data)
```

We get our `mnist.test.images`, which is equal to `mnist.train.images`, and extract the labels the same way, by calling the `expected` variable, and then we're going to compute `predicted` from the `classifier` model, using `classifier.predict(test_data)`. So, this is going to take just a little bit of time to execute. After execution, there should be no error messages, which indicates that our prediction ran successfully.

So, now we can see how well we did. We're going to use the built-in metrics functions from scikit-learn. We're going to record some of the metrics, such as *precision* and *recall*, and if you want to understand what those mean, I recommend the following Wikipedia article:

```
https://en.wikipedia.org/wiki/Precision_and_recall_to_understand_metric_
definitions
```

Just in short, they are different metrics for evaluating how well your machine learning algorithm did. Accuracy is probably the most common. It's simple: the correct data points divided by the total. But there's also precision recall that weighs the pros and cons with true positives, true negatives, false positives, and false negatives, and which one is the best depends on your application. It depends on which is worse between the false positive and the false negative and so forth and, on top of that, we're going to output what's known as a confusion matrix, which tells you which ones were successful and which ones were misclassified. Let's run the following code:

```
# And display the results
print("See https://en.wikipedia.org/wiki/Precision_and_recall to understand
metric definitions")
print("Classification report for classifier %s:\n%s\n"
      % (classifier, metrics.classification_report(expected, predicted)))
print("Confusion matrix:\n%s" % metrics.confusion_matrix(expected,
predicted))

images_and_predictions = list(zip(test_data, predicted))
for index, (image, prediction) in enumerate(images_and_predictions[:4]):
    plt.subplot(2, 4, index + 5)
    plt.axis('off')
    plt.imshow(image.reshape((28,28)), cmap=plt.cm.gray_r,
interpolation='nearest')
    plt.title('Prediction: %i' % prediction)

plt.show()
```

It should give us the following output:

```
See https://en.wikipedia.org/wiki/Precision_and_recall to understand metric definitions
Classification report for classifier SVC(C=1.0, cache_size=200, class_weight=None, coef0=0.0,
  decision_function_shape='ovr', degree=3, gamma=0.001, kernel='rbf',
  max_iter=-1, probability=False, random_state=None, shrinking=True,
  tol=0.001, verbose=False):
             precision    recall  f1-score   support

          0       0.96      0.99      0.97       980
          1       0.96      0.99      0.97      1135
          2       0.94      0.92      0.93      1032
          3       0.92      0.94      0.93      1010
          4       0.92      0.95      0.94       982
          5       0.93      0.90      0.91       892
          6       0.94      0.96      0.95       958
          7       0.95      0.93      0.94      1028
          8       0.93      0.91      0.92       974
          9       0.94      0.91      0.92      1009

  micro avg       0.94      0.94      0.94     10000
  macro avg       0.94      0.94      0.94     10000
weighted avg      0.94      0.94      0.94     10000


Confusion matrix:
[[ 967    0    1    0    0    5    5    1    1    0]
 [   0 1118    2    3    0    1    3    1    7    0]
 [   9    1  951   10   12    1   15    9   22    2]
 [   0    2   16  947    1   17    1   11   11    4]
 [   1    2    7    0  931    0    8    2    3   28]
 [   7    5    5   34    8  804   12    2   10    5]
 [   9    3    4    1    6   11  923    0    1    0]
 [   2   14   21    5    9    0    0  953    3   21]
 [   4    7    7   15    8   24   10    7  889    3]
 [  10    7    0   12   33    6    1   14    6  920]]

Prediction: 7  Prediction: 2  Prediction: 1  Prediction: 0

7 2 / 0
```

OK, so we get the classification reports and we can see `precision`, `recall`, and another metric called `f1-score` that you can read about in that same Wikipedia article. In short, zero is the worst case and one is the best case. In the preceding screenshot, we can see `precision`, `recall`, and `f1-score` for the different digits and we can see we're in the 90% range; it varies, which is OK. It depends on your application, but that might be good enough or that might be abysmally bad. It depends. We're actually going to see how we can do better a little later on using a more powerful model. We can see that it generally worked. We look at the confusion matrix here, where the columns tell you what the actual value is and the rows tell you what the predicted value is. Ideally, we would see all large values along the diagonal and all zeroes otherwise. There's always going to be some errors, we're human beings so that's going to happen but like I said, we're going to see if we can do a little bit better, in vast majority of cases it did work. Now, we can see some example random outputs, where we had some digits as follows:

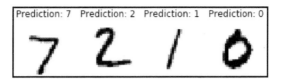

As we can see, all of the predictions are correct according to their images. OK, that's all well and good but I kind of feel like I'm taking the computer's word for it at this point. I'd like to throw my own data at it. I'd like to see how well this is really working, and this is something generally recommended with machine learning. You want to test it with your own data to really know if it's working and, if nothing else, it's much more satisfying. So, here is a little snippet of code that's going to use Jupyter's widget capabilities, its interactive capabilities:

```
#Let's test our model on images we draw ourselves!

from matplotlib.lines import Line2D
%pylab notebook
#This is needed for plot widgets

class Annotator(object):
    def __init__(self, axes):
        self.axes = axes

        self.xdata = []
        self.ydata = []
        self.xy = []
        self.drawon = False

    def mouse_move(self, event):
        if not event.inaxes:
            return

        x, y = event.xdata, event.ydata
        if self.drawon:
            self.xdata.append(x)
            self.ydata.append(y)
            self.xy.append((int(x),int(y)))
            line = Line2D(self.xdata,self.ydata)
            line.set_color('r')
            self.axes.add_line(line)

            plt.draw()

    def mouse_release(self, event):
        # Erase x and y data for new line
        self.xdata = []
```

```
        self.ydata = []
        self.drawon = False
    def mouse_press(self, event):
        self.drawon = True


img = np.zeros((28,28,3),dtype='uint8')

fig, axes = plt.subplots(figsize=(3,3))
axes.imshow(img)
plt.axis("off")
plt.gray()
annotator = Annotator(axes)
plt.connect('motion_notify_event', annotator.mouse_move)
plt.connect('button_release_event', annotator.mouse_release)
plt.connect('button_press_event', annotator.mouse_press)

axes.plot()

plt.show()
```

So, now we're actually going to create a little drawing widget. It's going to let us produce our own digits. Let's look at the code.

Let's import Line2D from matpllotlib.line, this is going to let us draw individual lines, like creating a kind of a vector image based on our mouse movements:

```
#Let's test our model on images we draw ourselves!

from matplotlib.lines import Line2D
```

We execute %pylab notebook; the percent sign indicates the following magic command:

```
%pylab notebook
```

It's kind of a meta command within Jupyter and Pylab Notebook, and it loads a bunch of stuff into your namespace for plotting and numerics. It's not necessary because we already did that with NumPy and Matplotlib, but to enable the widgets, we use this command.

Then, create this Annotator class, which contains call back for what happens if we move a mouse over our displayed image, as follows:

```
class Annotator(object):
    def __init__(self, axes):
        self.axes = axes

        self.xdata = []
        self.ydata = []
```

```
            self.xy = []
            self.drawon = False

    def mouse_move(self, event):
        if not event.inaxes:
            return

        x, y = event.xdata, event.ydata
        if self.drawon:
            self.xdata.append(x)
            self.ydata.append(y)
            self.xy.append((int(x),int(y)))
            line = Line2D(self.xdata,self.ydata)
            line.set_color('r')
            self.axes.add_line(line)

            plt.draw()

    def mouse_release(self, event):
        # Erase x and y data for new line
        self.xdata = []
        self.ydata = []
        self.drawon = False
    def mouse_press(self, event):
        self.drawon = True
```

We don't have to understand the `Annotator` class, but this might be something useful in the future if you want to make an annotation or draw something, and to seize a full snippet of code.

Then, we're going to create a blank image, the same size as our images. It's just going to be three RGBs for the time being. It just looks a little bit nicer, even though we're going to make it black and white in the end, because that's what our data is. Create the image as follows:

```
img = np.zeros((28,28,3),dtype='uint8')
```

Now, create a plot, show it, and hook up our `annotator` functions to that, as follows:

```
fig, axes = plt.subplots(figsize=(3,3))
axes.imshow(img)
plt.axis("off")
plt.gray()
annotator = Annotator(axes)
plt.connect('motion_notify_event', annotator.mouse_move)
plt.connect('button_release_event', annotator.mouse_release)
plt.connect('button_press_event', annotator.mouse_press)
```

```
axes.plot()

plt.show()
```

After running the code, we should get the following output:

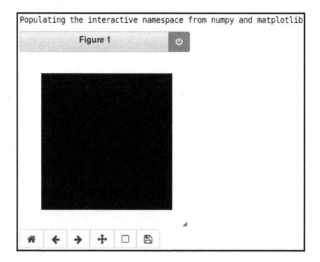

So, let's draw, say, the numeral three:

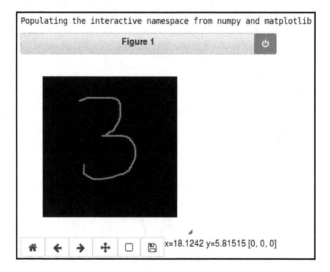

Now, that's sluggish you know, and isn't exactly going to replace Photoshop, but this still beats going into a separate program and creating your image file, making sure it's in the right format, saving it, and then writing code to load it and get it right. So, this will allow us to quickly play and experiment with our models. We just created a kind of array of lines, so we need to rasterize that and process it so that it looks more like actual handwritten digits, something that would come from either a scanned pencil drawing or a pressure-sensitive tablet. The following will do this:

```
# Now we see how our model "sees" (predicts the digit from)
# our hand drawn image...
# First, we rasterize (convert to pixels) our vector data
# and process the image to more closely resemble something
# drawn with a pencil or pressure-sensitive tablet.

digimg = np.zeros((28,28,3),dtype='uint8')
for ind, points in enumerate(annotator.xy[:-1]):
    digimg=cv2.line(digimg, annotator.xy[ind],
annotator.xy[ind+1],(255,0,0),1)
digimg = cv2.GaussianBlur(digimg,(5,5),1.0)
digimg = (digimg.astype('float')
*1.0/np.amax(digimg)).astype('float')[:,:,0]
digimg **= 0.5; digimg[digimg>0.9]=1.0

#The model is expecting the input in a particular format
testim = digimg.reshape((-1,28*28))

print("Support vector machine prediction:",classifier.predict( testim ))

outimg = testim.reshape((28,28))
figure(figsize=(3,3)); imshow(outimg);
```

Let's look at the code. First, we create a blank image, as follows:

```
digimg = np.zeros((28,28,3),dtype='uint8')
```

We iterate over the xy pairs that came from our annotator and then we're going to draw lines there in raster format on our rasterized images, as follows:

```
for ind, points in enumerate(annotator.xy[:-1]):
    digimg=cv2.line(digimg, annotator.xy[ind],
annotator.xy[ind+1],(255,0,0),1)
digimg = cv2.GaussianBlur(digimg,(5,5),1.0)
```

Then, we convert the image to a `float`, from range 0 to 1, just like our input data, as follows:

```
digimg = (digimg.astype('float')
*1.0/np.amax(digimg)).astype('float')[:,:,0]
```

Then, we are going to bring it a little bit closer to 1, because that's just what our input images look like and what our model would be expecting:

```
digimg **= 0.5; digimg[digimg>0.9]=1.0
```

Then, we have our two-dimensional image but, of course, to run it through our model, we need to flatten it into 1 x 784, so that's what this `reshape` function does:

```
#The model is expecting the input in a particular format
testim = digimg.reshape((-1,28*28))
```

Then, we're going to run that through our `classifier` and print the output as well. We will create a figure where we can see what our rasterized image looks like, as follows:

```
print("Support vector machine prediction:",classifier.predict( testim ))

outimg = testim.reshape((28,28))
figure(figsize=(3,3)); imshow(outimg);
```

We should get the following output:

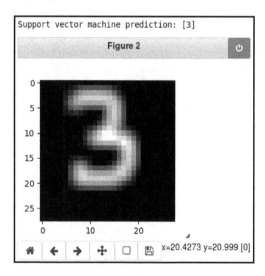

We drew a three and we predicted a 3. Excellent. Let's try something else. Clear the previous output by hitting *Ctrl + Enter*, and we get a warning message; it's just telling us that it has clobbered some of the variables that were created. That's not a big deal. You can safely ignore that. Just a fair warning, your mileage may vary on this, depending on what your handwriting is like and what was in your training data. If you wanted this to work perfectly every time, or as close to that as possible, you want to train it probably on your own handwriting.

Let's try a zero:

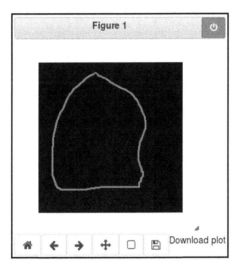

The following is the output:

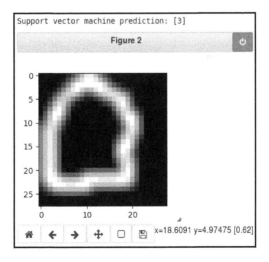

So, here you can see an example of it not working. The prediction is supposed to be zero but the model predicted a three for some reason. It's possible that if you redraw it, it might work. So, again, your mileage may vary. Experiment with it. You can also play with the preprocessing, although this, as far as I can tell, works pretty well. But anyway, we can see that our model is, at least for the most part, working. So, that's going to be it for the scikit-learn support vector machines. Now, in our next section, we're going to introduce TensorFlow and perform digit classification with that.

Introducing TensorFlow with digit classification

We're going to see TensorFlow in action and see how we can perform digit classification with a tractable amount of code. TensorFlow is Google's machine learning library, for numerical analysis in general. It is called TensorFlow because it supposedly flows tensors, where tensors are defined to be arrays of *n* dimensions. Tensors have a real geometric meaning that just multidimensional arrays don't necessarily classify, but we're just going to use that term. A tensor is just a multidimensional array.

Here, we're going to do a simple `softmax` example. It's a very simple model; you can visit TensorFlow's own website (https://www.tensorflow.org/get_started/mnist/beginners) for more information. Let's have a look at the following code:

```
data_dir = '/tmp/tensorflow/mnist/input_data'
mnist = input_data.read_data_sets(data_dir, one_hot=True)
# Create the model
x = tf.placeholder(tf.float32, [None, 784])
W = tf.Variable(tf.zeros([784, 10]))
b = tf.Variable(tf.zeros([10]))
y = tf.matmul(x, W) + b
# Define loss and optimizer
y_ = tf.placeholder(tf.float32, [None, 10])
cross_entropy = tf.reduce_mean(
  tf.nn.softmax_cross_entropy_with_logits(labels=y_, logits=y))
train_step = tf.train.GradientDescentOptimizer(0.5).minimize(cross_entropy)
sess = tf.InteractiveSession()
tf.global_variables_initializer().run()
# Train
for _ in range(1000):
    batch_xs, batch_ys = mnist.train.next_batch(100)
    sess.run(train_step, feed_dict={x: batch_xs, y_: batch_ys})
# Test trained model
correct_prediction = tf.equal(tf.argmax(y, 1), tf.argmax(y_, 1))
```

```
accuracy = tf.reduce_mean(tf.cast(correct_prediction, tf.float32))
print(\"Model accuracy:\",sess.run(accuracy, feed_dict={x:
mnist.test.images,
                              y_: mnist.test.labels}))
```

In short, you're going to take your input data and you're going to multiply it by a matrix. The data has 784 points. Each point is going to have a matrix value and, for each of the 10 classes, you're going to compute an inner product by multiplying 784 × 784 and sum them up. There will be 10 outputs. It will be a 1 by 10 array, and you're going to add a bias variable to the output of the array and run it through the softmax function, which will convert it to something. The output of the matrix plus the bias will compute something in the range of 0 to 1, which loosely corresponds to the probability of that data being in that class. For example, there might be a 0.4% probability or 40% probability of being a 1, a 2% probability of being it 2, and 90% probability of it being a 9, and the output is going to be the maximum output of that.

TensorFlow is very sophisticated. There's a little bit more setup here than there was with the scikit-learn example. You can learn more about that on their own website. Now, let's go through the following code in detail:

```
data_dir = '/tmp/tensorflow/mnist/input_data'
mnist = input_data.read_data_sets(data_dir, one_hot=True)
```

We've already done this in the previous example. Now, we're going to get the data from data_dir; make sure it's in our mnist variable.

Then, we create the model where x corresponds to our input data and, although we're not loading the data just yet, we just need to create a placeholder so TensorFlow knows where stuff is. We don't need to know how many examples there are, and that's what the None dimension corresponds to, but we do need to know how big each example is, which in this case is 784. W is the matrix that's going to multiply x classes to the inner product over the image, 784 *dot* 784, and you do that 10 times. So, that corresponds to a 784/10 matrix, 10 being the number of classes; then, you add the b bias variable to that. The values of W and b are what TensorFlow is going to produce for us based on our inputs, and y defines the actual operation that's going to be performed on our data from the matrix multiplication. We add the b bias variable to it as follows:

```
x = tf.placeholder(tf.float32, [None, 784])
W = tf.Variable(tf.zeros([784, 10]))
b = tf.Variable(tf.zeros([10]))
y = tf.matmul(x, W) + b
```

We need to create a placeholder for our labeled data, as follows:

```
y_ = tf.placeholder(tf.float32, [None, 10])
```

In order to do machine learning, you need a `loss` function or a `fitness` function, which tells you how well your model is doing given learning parameters like those given in `W` and `b`. Hence, we're going to use something called `cross-entropy`; we'll not go into much detail about `cross-entropy` but that's going to give us some criteria for letting us know that we're getting closer to a working model, as shown in the following lines of code:

```
cross_entropy = tf.reduce_mean(
    tf.nn.softmax_cross_entropy_with_logits(labels=y_, logits=y))
train_step = tf.train.GradientDescentOptimizer(0.5).minimize(cross_entropy)
```

As we add more and more data, we're going to use what's known as `GradientDescentOptimizer` in order to minimize the error, minimize the cross entropy, and make our model fit as well as possible.

In the following code, we're actually going to start by creating an interactive session, as follows:

```
sess = tf.InteractiveSession()
tf.global_variables_initializer().run()
for _ in range(1000):
    batch_xs, batch_ys = mnist.train.next_batch(100)
    sess.run(train_step, feed_dict={x: batch_xs, y_: batch_ys})
```

We want to make it an interactive session so that we can use our model and buy new data to it afterwards. We're going to initialize `run()` and then we're going to compute the data in batches. TensorFlow is a very powerful program and it allows you to break up your data. We're not going to do it here, but you can run parallelized code fairly easily with it. Here, we're just going to iterate `1000` times and compete stuff in batches feeding in our training data.

After this runs, we're going to see how well we did and just see where our predicted data is equal to the given labels to it. We can compute the `accuracy` by just seeing how many of the predictions were correct on average. Then, print that data, as follows:

```
correct_prediction = tf.equal(tf.argmax(y, 1), tf.argmax(y_, 1))
accuracy = tf.reduce_mean(tf.cast(correct_prediction, tf.float32))
print(\"Model accuracy:\",sess.run(accuracy, feed_dict={x:
mnist.test.images,
                                    y_: mnist.test.labels}))
```

The following is the output:

```
Extracting /tmp/tensorflow/mnist/input_data/train-images-idx3-ubyte.gz
Extracting /tmp/tensorflow/mnist/input_data/train-labels-idx1-ubyte.gz
Extracting /tmp/tensorflow/mnist/input_data/t10k-images-idx3-ubyte.gz
Extracting /tmp/tensorflow/mnist/input_data/t10k-labels-idx1-ubyte.gz
WARNING:tensorflow:From <ipython-input-18-b2f1671e64b3>:16: softmax_cross_entropy_with_logits (from tensorflow.python.op
s.nn_ops) is deprecated and will be removed in a future version.
Instructions for updating:

Future major versions of TensorFlow will allow gradients to flow
into the labels input on backprop by default.

See tf.nn.softmax_cross_entropy_with_logits_v2.

Model accuracy: 0.918
```

Being a really simple model, it runs a lot faster and we can see that we got a little less than 92% accuracy. The code executed a lot faster, but a little bit less accurately than our **Support Vector Machine** (**SVM**), but that's OK. This code just provides a very simple example of how TensorFlow works.

You get a little bit more advanced momentarily, but let's test the following code the way we did before:

```
img = np.zeros((28,28,3),dtype='uint8')
fig, axes = plt.subplots(figsize=(3,3))
axes.imshow(img)
plt.axis("off")
plt.gray()
annotator = Annotator(axes)
plt.connect('motion_notify_event', annotator.mouse_move)
plt.connect('button_release_event', annotator.mouse_release)
plt.connect('button_press_event', annotator.mouse_press)
axes.plot()
plt.show()
```

We get the following output:

Our annotator is initiated and let's put in a digit. Try a 3:

Now, we're going to preprocess the drawn digit and it's almost the same code as before, which is going to go through the classes and possible classes for our data and see which one the TensorFlow `softmax` model thought was the best:

```
for tindex in range(10):
    testlab = np.zeros((1,10))
    testlab[0,tindex] = 1
    if sess.run(accuracy, feed_dict={x: testim, y_ : testlab}) == 1:
        break
```

So, we'll run the preceding block and, as shown, it predicts a 3 from a 3:

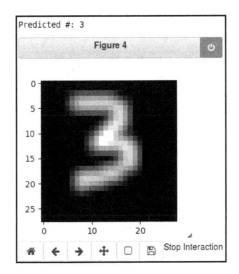

Sometimes it might not predict correctly, and that is unfortunately going to happen. So, there are two ways to improve that: train on your own handwriting or use a better model.

We are going to move on to the most powerful model in this section. Here, we're going to just briefly touch on deep learning with, **convolutional neural networks** (**CNNs**). We are not covering the theory here. There's a lot to know about deep learning and multi-layered neural networks in general. Deep learning is a deep subject but, for this chapter, we're just going to see how we can actually apply state-of-the-art machine learning techniques to digit recognition with a relatively simple block of code.

So, we have a deepnn(x) function here that creates our deep neural network, finds our hidden layers or convolutional layers, pools, and so forth, and defines all our necessary stuff from our input:

```
def deepnn(x):
    with tf.name_scope('reshape'):
    x_image = tf.reshape(x, [-1, 28, 28, 1])
```

`deepnn` builds the graph for a deep net for classifying digits and `reshape` function is to be used within a convolutional neural net. The arguments used here are:

- x: An input tensor with the dimensions (`N_examples`, `784`), where `784` is the number of pixels in a standard MNIST image.
- y: A tensor of shape (`N_examples`, `10`), with values equal to the logic's of classifying the digit into one of 10 classes (the digits 0-9). `keep_prob` is a scalar placeholder for the probability of dropout.

This returns a tuple (`y`, `keep_prob`). The last dimension is for *features*—there is only one here, since images are grayscale—it would be 3 for an RGB image, 4 for RGBA, and so on.

The first convolutional layer maps one grayscale image to `32` feature maps:

```
with tf.name_scope('conv1'):
W_conv1 = weight_variable([5, 5, 1, 32])
b_conv1 = bias_variable([32])
h_conv1 = tf.nn.relu(conv2d(x_image, W_conv1) + b_conv1)
# Pooling layer - downsamples by 2X.
with tf.name_scope('pool1'):
h_pool1 = max_pool_2x2(h_conv1)
# Second convolutional layer -- maps 32 feature maps to 64.
with tf.name_scope('conv2'):
W_conv2 = weight_variable([5, 5, 32, 64])
b_conv2 = bias_variable([64])
h_conv2 = tf.nn.relu(conv2d(h_pool1, W_conv2) + b_conv2)
# Second pooling layer.
with tf.name_scope('pool2'):
h_pool2 = max_pool_2x2(h_conv2)
# Fully connected layer 1 -- after 2 round of downsampling, our 28x28
image
# is down to 7x7x64 feature maps -- maps this to 1024 features.
with tf.name_scope('fc1'):
W_fc1 = weight_variable([7 * 7 * 64, 1024])
b_fc1 = bias_variable([1024])
h_pool2_flat = tf.reshape(h_pool2, [-1, 7*7*64])
h_fc1 = tf.nn.relu(tf.matmul(h_pool2_flat, W_fc1) + b_fc1)
# Dropout - controls the complexity of the model, prevents co-
adaptation of
# features.
with tf.name_scope('dropout'):
keep_prob = tf.placeholder(tf.float32)
h_fc1_drop = tf.nn.dropout(h_fc1, keep_prob)
# Map the 1024 features to 10 classes, one for each digit
with tf.name_scope('fc2'):
```

```
    W_fc2 = weight_variable([1024, 10])
    b_fc2 = bias_variable([10])
    y_conv = tf.matmul(h_fc1_drop, W_fc2) + b_fc2
    return y_conv, keep_prob
  def conv2d(x, W):
"""conv2d returns a 2d convolution layer with full stride."""
    return tf.nn.conv2d(x, W, strides=[1, 1, 1, 1], padding='SAME')
  def max_pool_2x2(x):
   """max_pool_2x2 downsamples a feature map by 2X."""
    return tf.nn.max_pool(x, ksize=[1, 2, 2, 1],
    strides=[1, 2, 2, 1], padding='SAME')
  def weight_variable(shape):
   """weight_variable generates a weight variable of a given shape."""
    initial = tf.truncated_normal(shape, stddev=0.1)
    return tf.Variable(initial)
  def bias_variable(shape):
   """bias_variable generates a bias variable of a given shape."""
    initial = tf.constant(0.1, shape=shape)
    return tf.Variable(initial)
```

We have our functions that do convolutions, weight variables, bias variables, and so forth. Then, we have our main code here:

```
  ###begin main code
  data_dir= '/tmp/tensorflow/mnist/input_data'
  # Import data
  mnist = input_data.read_data_sets(data_dir, one_hot=True)
  # Create the model
  x = tf.placeholder(tf.float32, [None, 784])
  # Define loss and optimizer
  y_ = tf.placeholder(tf.float32, [None, 10])
  # Build the graph for the deep net
  y_conv, keep_prob = deepnn(x)
  with tf.name_scope('loss'):
   cross_entropy = tf.nn.softmax_cross_entropy_with_logits(labels=y_,
   logits=y_conv)
  cross_entropy = tf.reduce_mean(cross_entropy)
  with tf.name_scope('adam_optimizer'):
   train_step = tf.train.AdamOptimizer(1e-4).minimize(cross_entropy)
  with tf.name_scope('accuracy'):
   correct_prediction = tf.equal(tf.argmax(y_conv, 1), tf.argmax(y_, 1))
   correct_prediction = tf.cast(correct_prediction, tf.float32)
   accuracy = tf.reduce_mean(correct_prediction)
  graph_location = tempfile.mkdtemp()
  print('Saving graph to: %s' % graph_location)
  train_writer = tf.summary.FileWriter(graph_location)
  train_writer.add_graph(tf.get_default_graph())
  # Let's run the model
```

```
sess = tf.InteractiveSession()
sess.run(tf.global_variables_initializer())
for i in range(20000):
 batch = mnist.train.next_batch(50)
 if i % 100 == 0:
 train_accuracy = accuracy.eval(feed_dict={
 x: batch[0], y_: batch[1], keep_prob: 1.0})
 print('step %d, training accuracy %g' % (i, train_accuracy))
 train_step.run(feed_dict={x: batch[0], y_: batch[1], keep_prob: 0.5})
# How did we do?
print('test accuracy %g' % accuracy.eval(feed_dict={
 x: mnist.test.images, y_: mnist.test.labels, keep_prob: 1.0}))
```

The mnist variable gets the data in case we don't already have it. We define our placeholder for the input, and the outputs build the graph. We then define the fitness function and cross-entropy and create our graph. We have to be careful while creating the session; in the example on their website, they just created a normal session. We want an interactive session here, so that we can apply our model to our own generated data, and we're going to break this up into batches. We'll run it, and every 100 iterations it's going to tell us what exactly it's doing and then, at the end, it will tell us our accuracy.

Let's run the code and extract the data, and you can see the statistics as follows:

```
Extracting /tmp/tensorflow/mnist/input_data/train-images-idx3-ubyte.gz
Extracting /tmp/tensorflow/mnist/input_data/train-labels-idx1-ubyte.gz
Extracting /tmp/tensorflow/mnist/input_data/t10k-images-idx3-ubyte.gz
Extracting /tmp/tensorflow/mnist/input_data/t10k-labels-idx1-ubyte.gz
Saving graph to: /tmp/tmpdr9rhjcj
step 0, training accuracy 0.1
step 100, training accuracy 0.86
step 200, training accuracy 0.92
step 300, training accuracy 0.94
step 400, training accuracy 0.94
step 500, training accuracy 0.92
step 600, training accuracy 0.9
step 700, training accuracy 0.88
step 800, training accuracy 0.92
step 900, training accuracy 0.96
```

It starts off with very bad training accuracy but it quickly gets up to over 90% and shoots up to 1. It's not exactly 100%, but that usually means it's something like 99%, so pretty close to 1. This usually takes a few minutes. OK, now we have created our TensorFlow classifier.

Evaluating the results

After we finished training, as we can see from the following screenshot, we get a result of over 99%, so that is significantly better than what we got with `softmax` or our SVM:

```
step 18500, training accuracy 1
step 18600, training accuracy 1
step 18700, training accuracy 1
step 18800, training accuracy 1
step 18900, training accuracy 1
step 19000, training accuracy 1
step 19100, training accuracy 1
step 19200, training accuracy 1
step 19300, training accuracy 1
step 19400, training accuracy 1
step 19500, training accuracy 1
step 19600, training accuracy 1
step 19700, training accuracy 1
step 19800, training accuracy 1
step 19900, training accuracy 1
test accuracy 0.9933
```

Deep learning is probably the most powerful machine learning technique, due to its ability to learn very complex pattern recognition. It's just dominating everything else for advanced computer vision, speech processing, and more—stuff that conventional machine learning techniques haven't been all that successful at. However, that doesn't necessarily mean that you want to use deep learning for everything. Deep learning generally acquires a large number of examples—many thousands, if not millions sometimes—and it can also be very computationally expensive. So, it's not always the best solution, although it is very powerful, as we have seen right here. So, 99% is about as good as you can get.

The following is the code to draw digits:

```
# Test on handwritten digits again
img = np.zeros((28,28,3),dtype='uint8')
fig, axes = plt.subplots(figsize=(3,3))
axes.imshow(img)
plt.axis("off")
plt.gray()
annotator = Annotator(axes)
plt.connect('motion_notify_event', annotator.mouse_move)
plt.connect('button_release_event', annotator.mouse_release)
plt.connect('button_press_event', annotator.mouse_press)
axes.plot()
plt.show()
```

The following code rasterizes and preprocesses the handwritten digit image:

```
# Rasterize and preprocess the above
digimg = np.zeros((28,28,3),dtype='uint8')
for ind, points in enumerate(annotator.xy[:-1]):
    digimg=cv2.line(digimg, annotator.xy[ind],
annotator.xy[ind+1],(255,0,0),1)
digimg = cv2.GaussianBlur(digimg,(5,5),1.0)
digimg = (digimg.astype('float')
*1.0/np.amax(digimg)).astype('float')[:,:,0]
digimg **= 0.5; digimg[digimg>0.9]=1.0
testim = digimg.reshape((-1,28*28))

# And run through our model
for tindex in range(10):
    testlab = np.zeros((1,10))
    testlab[0,tindex] = 1
    if accuracy.eval(feed_dict={x: testim, y_: testlab,
                               keep_prob: 1.0}) == 1:
        break

print("Predicted #:",tindex) #tindex = TF model prediction

# Display our rasterized digit
outimg = testim.reshape((28,28))
figure(figsize=(3,3)); imshow(outimg)
```

So, let's test it again on our handwritten digit 0:

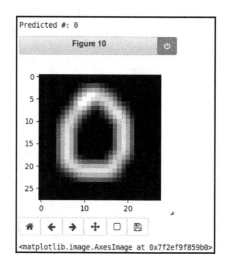

Again, we have similar code for processing the vectorized image, and we're getting the output and raster form and running it through our model, doing `accuracy.eval` here. As we can see in the preceding screenshot, we've got a zero as expected, and that's perfect. So, we're going to be talking more about deep learning with CNNs in the next chapters, but we've already seen how powerful it is with relatively little code and we were able to fly it towards our particular problem of digit recognition. Alright, so, with that, we're going to move on to our next chapter, which is `Chapter 6`, *Facial Feature Tracking and Classification with dlib*.

Summary

In this chapter, we learned how to perform digit classification with TensorFlow using `softmax`. We learned how to acquire and process MNIST digit data. We then learned how to create and train a support vector machine, and apply it to new data.

In the next chapter, we will learn facial feature tracking and classification using dlib.

6
Facial Feature Tracking and Classification with dlib

In this chapter, we'll learn about dlib and how to locate faces from images and videos with the help of some examples. We will also learn about facial recognition using dlib.

We are going to cover the following topics:

- Introducing dlib
- Facial landmarks
- Finding 68 facial landmarks in images
- Faces in videos
- Facial recognition

Introducing dlib

dlib is a general-purpose, cross-platform software library written in the programming language C++. We are going to learn dlib and understand how to find and use human facial features from images and videos. According to their own website, dlib.net, dlib is a modern C++ tool containing machine learning algorithms and tools for creating complex software in C++ to solve real-world problems. It is a C++ toolkit and, just like OpenCV, it contains a very nice set of Python bindings that will work very well for our applications.

dlib is a very rich library and contains a whole lot of algorithms and features, which are very well documented on their website. This makes it easy to learn from, and it has a whole lot of examples similar to what we're going to do in this chapter and for your customized projects. It is recommended that you check their website if you're interested in dlib and want to learn how to use it for your applications. The *High Quality Portable Code* section on the `http://dlib.net/` website has efficient code for Microsoft Windows, Linux, and macOS, and just like Python, contains a very rich set of machine learning algorithms, including state-of-the-art deep learning, which we are using in this chapter, although we're going to use TensorFlow for our purposes. It also has **Support Vector Machines** (**SVMs**), which we saw in `Chapter 5`, *Handwritten Digit Recognition with scikit-learn and TensorFlow* on handwritten digit recognition, and a wide variety of other things for object detection and clustering, K-means, and so forth. It also has a rich set of numerical algorithms, linear algebra, **singular value decomposition** (**SVD**), and a whole lot optimization algorithms, as well as graphical model inference algorithms, and image processing (which is very useful for us). It has routines for reading and writing common image formats (although we won't use them as we're going to use the tools that we've already seen for reading and writing images) and **Speeded-Up Robust Features** (**SURF**), **Histogram of Oriented Gradient** (**HOG**), and FHOG, which are useful for image detection and recognition. What's interesting for now are the tools for detecting objects, including frontal face detection, pose estimation, and facial feature recognition. So, we'll talk about that in this chapter. There are some other features of dlib, such as threading, networking, **Graphical User Interface** (**GUI**) development, data compression, and a bunch of other utilities. `http://dlib.net/` includes examples in C++ and examples in Python. What we're going to be interested in is face detection, facial landmark detection, and recognition. So, we're going to go through similar examples to see what we have here.

Facial landmarks

We're going to learn all about facial landmarks in dlib. Before we can run any code, we need to grab some data that's used for facial features themselves. We'll see what these facial features are and exactly what details we're looking for. This is not included with Python dlib distributions, so you will have to download this. We'll go to the `dlib.net/files/` site, where you can see all the source code files; scroll to the bottom and you can see the `shape_predictor_68_face_landmarks.dat.bz2` file. Click on it and then save it wherever you keep your Jupyter Notebooks for this book.

Okay, so, what exactly is that? What are these 68 landmarks? Well, these landmarks are a common feature set that was generated by training alpha datasets from something called iBUG (`https://ibug.doc.ic.ac.uk/resources/facial-point-annotations/`), the intelligent behavior understanding group. So, this is a pre-trained model, a database of a whole bunch of human faces of people from all over the world, male/female, different age groups, and so forth.

So, we'll work on a variety of cases, and what we're looking for is a bunch of points around the outline of the face, as you can see in the following diagram:

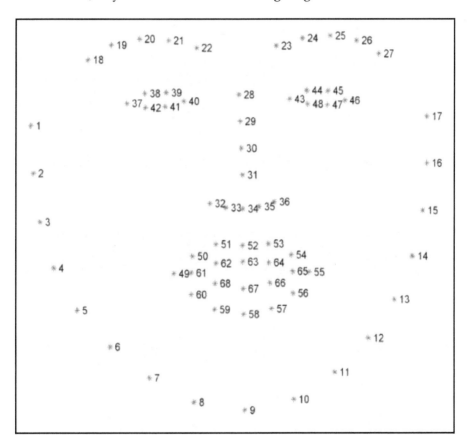

Points **1** through **17** are the outline of the face, points **18** through **22** are the right eyebrow, **23** to **27** the left eyebrow, **28** to **31** the ridge of the nose, **30** to **36** the base of the nose, **37** to **42** forms the right eye, and **43** to **48** outlines the left eye, and then there are a whole bunch of points for the mouth, including both sides of the upper lip and both sides of the lower lip.

So, these are common features that all human faces will have, and this will allow us to do a whole lot of things like facial recognition and identification, pose estimation, possibly age estimation, gender estimation, and even neat things like facial stitching and facial blending. A lot of very interesting things can be done just with this information, and these are just based on pure intensity values on the face. So, there are no SURF features, **Scale Invariant Feature Transform** (**SIFT**) features, HOG features, or anything like that. These are just detectable from pixel values. So, effectively you can convert from RGB to black and white to monochrome, and you can run this model if it's an ensemble of regression trees.

You can download the iBUG dataset and train your own model, and you can actually vary the number of features. There are datasets with more features than this, but this is more than adequate for our purposes. You can train it if you want to run it on a variety of faces or particular faces, but you'll find that this pre-trained dataset is going to work in a wide variety of cases. So, iBUG is powerful in and of itself. We're going to use it here, and we're going to see how to run the code that will find all these features for some images and for some videos. Then, we're going to apply that to the facial recognition problem, where we differentiate between faces in a given set. After you have downloaded the `shape_predictor_68_face_landmarks.dat.bz2` file, you can put the file in your directory where you have your Jupyter Notebook and with that, we can get started with our code.

Finding 68 facial landmarks in images

In this section, we're going to see our first example, where we find 68 facial landmarks and images with single people and with multiple people. So, let's open our Jupyter Notebook for this section. Take a look at this first cell:

```
%pylab notebook

import dlib
import cv2
import os
import tkinter
from tkinter import filedialog
from IPython import display
root = tkinter.Tk()
root.withdraw()
#Go to your working directory (will be different for you)
%cd /home/test/13293
```

We've got to do some basic setup, as we did in the previous chapters. We're going to initialize `%pylab notebook`. Again, that will load NumPy and PyPlot and some other stuff, and we're going to perform `notebook` for now, which will be good for close-up views of images, though we're going to switch it to `inline` for the second example because we'll need that for looking at videos. Then, we have to import our other libraries. dlib is the focus of this section, of course.

We're going to use a few utilities from OpenCV, but it's just additional annotation and working with videos. We're going to use `tkinter` so we have a nice file dialog display. So, rather than hardcoding the filename into our code, we'll just prompt the user for the file that we want to analyze. We'll import `display` from IPython in order to watch the movie for the second example, and we have to set up `tkinter`; we want to make sure that we're in the working directory with all our files. You might not need this, but you can do it just to be sure.

So, we're going to select the cell, hit *Ctrl + Enter*, and then, if everything worked correctly, you should see the following output:

```
Populating the interactive namespace from numpy and matplotlib
/home/test/13293
```

You can see `Populating the interactive namespace` and your current working directory.

Okay, so let's see the first example now that we're set up, and we'll actually use those 68 features from that file that we downloaded; we'll see how easy it is to do this within dlib. Now, we're going to see that this is only just a little bit of code, but it does something really cool:

```
imgname = filedialog.askopenfilename(parent = root,initialdir =
os.getcwd(), title = 'Select image file...')
img = imread(imgname)
img.flags['WRITEABLE']=True

annotated = img.copy()

predictor_path = "./shape_predictor_68_face_landmarks.dat"

detector = dlib.get_frontal_face_detector()

predictor = dlib.shape_predictor(predictor_path)
font = cv2.FONT_HERSHEY_SIMPLEX

dets = detector(img, 1)
```

```
print("Number of faces detected: {}".format(len(dets)))
for k, d in enumerate(dets):
    print("Detection {}: Left: {} Top: {} Right: {} Bottom: {}".format(k,
d.left(), d.top(), d.right(), d.bottom()))
    shape = predictor(img,d)
    print("Part 0: {}, Part 1:{} ...".format(shape.part(0),shape.part(1)))
    head_width = shape.part(16).x-shape.part(0).y
    fontsize = head_width/650
    for pt in range(68):
        x,y = shape.part(pt).x, shape.part(pt).y
        annotated = cv2.putText(annotated, str(pt), (x,y), font, fontsize,
(255,255,255),2, cv2.LINE_AA)
figure(figsize = (8,6))
imshow(annotated)
```

First, we're going to ask the user for the filename. So, this is using `tkinter` and we're going to open a filename; it'll start searching in the current working directory using the `initialdir=os.getcwd()` function:

```
imgname = filedialog.askopenfilename(parent = root,initialdir =
os.getcwd(), title = 'Select image file...')
```

We'll read that in using the following line:

```
img = imread(imgname)
img.flags['WRITEABLE']=True
```

The `img.flags['WRITEABLE']=True` line is kind of a quirk of dlib, not really a big deal but, depending on how you loaded the file, `flags` for a `WRITEABLE` might be set `False`. That happens with `imread`. It depends on how you load it, but just to be sure, `WRITEABLE` needs to be set to `True`. Otherwise, dlib will throw an error. Depending on how you load, this might not be necessary.

We want to create an image that we can write on, where we can actually display where the landmarks were found, so we're going to create a copy of our image that we loaded earlier, the image that has the face in it, so we can write to it without clobbering the original image:

```
annotated = img.copy()
```

Now, we will load the data from the file we downloaded. `shape_predictor_68_face_landmarks.dat.bz2` comes in `.bz2` format; if you have not already unzipped it, you can unzip it to the `.dat` format. If you're on Windows, then it is recommend to use 7-zip. If you're on Linux or macOS, there should be a built-in utility you can just double-click on and it should be pretty straightforward to extract that.

So, we'll set the path and keep it in the current directory, and we need to initialize our objects:

```
predictor_path = "./shape_predictor_68_face_landmarks.dat"
```

Now, there are two stages here. First, you need to detect where the faces are. This is similar to what Haar cascades would do if you've used OpenCV and those examples before, but we use dlib.get_frontal_face_detector, which is just built-in:

```
detector = dlib.get_frontal_face_detector()
```

So, we create the detector object, get it from dlib.get_frontal_face_detector, initialize that, and then there's the predictor:

```
predictor = dlib.shape_predictor(predictor_path)
```

Once we've detected where the face is, we know how many faces there are, and there can be more than one. dlib works fine for multiple faces, as we'll see. Once you know where the faces are, then you can run the predictor, which actually finds where those 68 landmarks previously mentioned are. So, we create our detector object and our predictor object, again making sure predictor_path is set up correctly.

Then, we'll set our font here:

```
font = cv2.FONT_HERSHEY_SIMPLEX
```

font is just displaying landmark data on the annotated image. So, you can change that if you want. Okay, now we get to the fun part of the code. First, do the detection, and find where exactly the faces are. Here's one really simple line of code:

```
dets = detector(img,1)
```

We're going to just print out the number of faces detected:

```
print("Number of faces detected: {}".format(len(dets)))
```

This can be useful for debugging purposes, although we'll see the output image where it actually detected the faces.

Now, we're going to do a for loop here, and this will handle the case where we could have more than one face:

```
#1 detection = 1 face; iterate over them and display data
for k, d in enumerate(dets):
```

So, we're going to iterate over each one. The length of det s could be one, more than one, or zero, but we're not going to do that in this case. If you're not sure, then you might want to put this in a try...catch block, but we're only going to deal with images that have visible faces here.

So, we'll iterate over the faces, and display where exactly the bounding box is for each face on the Left, Top, Right, and Bottom; where exactly did those go? Note the following code:

```
print("Detection {}: Left: {} Top:{} Right: {} Bottom: {}".format(
    k, d.left(), d.top(), d.right(), d.bottom())))
```

This is where the magic happens:

```
shape = predictor(img, d)
```

We're going to find the shape, then we're going to find those 68 landmarks, and just do a sanity check by printing out the first couple of landmarks just to make sure that it's working:

```
print("Part 0: {}, Part 1: {} ...".format(shape.part(0), shape.part(1)))
```

Okay, so, we have our landmarks for the face, and now we want to actually display it to understand what exactly we have here. We want to scale the font to make sure that fits the image because, depending on the size of the image, you could have a high resolution such as a 4,000 × 2,000 image, or you could have a low resolution such as a 300 × 200 (or something similar) and the heads could be very large in the image, as if the subject is close to the camera, or the reverse, small if it's far away.

So, we want to scale our font to the size of the head in the image:

```
#We want to scale the font to be in proportion to the head
#pts 16 and 0 correspond to the extreme points on the right/left side of
head
head_width = shape.part(16).x-shape.part(0).x
fontsize = head_width/650
```

So, here we're just computing head_width. shape is a predictor object that has a part method, and you pass in the index of the landmark that you want to find and each landmark is going to have an x and a y part. So, head_width is 16 here, which is dependent on your perspective. head_width is just width in terms of pixels of the head. Then, we're going to scale the font size based on head_width, and 650 is just a nice factor that works well.

Now, we have all the data, we're going to iterate over each of the points:

```
for pt in range(68);
    x,y = shape.part(pt).x, shape.part(pt).y
    annotated=cv2.putText(annotated, str(pt), (x,y), font, fontsize,
(255,255,255),2, cv2.LINE_AA)
```

So, we'll hardcode `68`, because we know that we have `68` points, but if you were using another kind of shape finder, such as a pre-trained shape finder, then you might want to change this number. We iterate over the points and then we get the x and the y coordinates for each of the landmarks that were shown before. We extract the x and y coordinates using `shape.part` and update the annotated image. We need `cv2` to put the text into the image. dlib does have something similar to this, but `cv2` is better, and we can have just one interface for that anyway. So, we're going to use OpenCV here and then we're going to create a figure and display it:

```
figure(figsize=(8,6))
imshow(annotated)
```

So, that's all regarding the code, and hopefully that seems pretty straightforward to you. Read it at your leisure. When we execute the code, we can see a dialog box of stock photos. We can select any photo among those; for instance, here is the photo of a man wearing a hat. So, it'll take just a little bit to compute that, and here you go:

We see this guy with all 68 points. We have labeled it from **0** to **67**, because of Python's index from **0** convention, but we can see that, just like before, we have all of the points; so, you can see point **0** on the left side, point **16** on the right side, depending on your perspective, and then it continues all the way around. Here's a zoomed view for clarity:

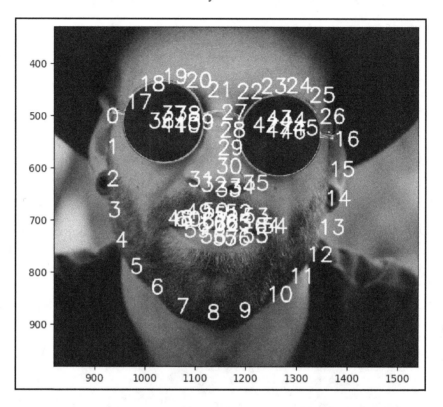

As we can see, some of the points are close together, but you can get the idea here of what's what. It looks pretty clear. So, this is pretty cool, and there's a whole lot you can do with this, as mentioned before. This guy is looking straight into the camera, so you might be asking what happens if somebody has their head tilted? Alright, we're going to run this again.

Let's select the stock photo woman here:

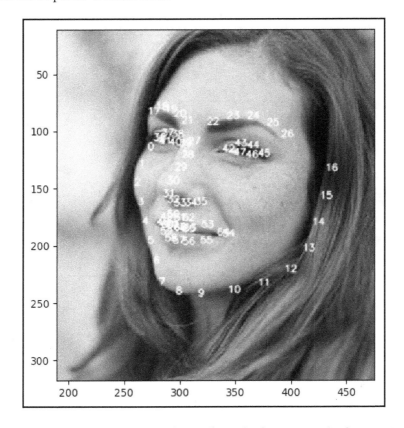

You can see her head is turned, and yet this still works fine. It won't always work in extreme cases; if somebody's head is turned so much that landmarks aren't there, then this can fail for reasonable cases, you can see that this actually works very nicely.

Okay, so what about multiple faces? Does this work for that? Let's have a look at another group photo:

We can see we have six people here in various poses. Given the resolution here, it's not possible to read those annotations, but that's perfectly okay because you have seen where they are, and we can see that we actually detected all six faces very nicely. So, hopefully you can get some ideas here of how you can use this in your own code, and just how easy dlib makes it for you in terms of detection phases.

Faces in videos

We're going to see our second example from what we learned in the last section on faces in photos. The still image example was neat, but you might be asking about videos. Okay, let's look at that for our next example:

```
%pylab inline
%cd /home/test/13293
import dlib
import cv2
import os
import tkinter
from tkinter import filedialog
from IPython import display
root = tkinter.Tk()
root.withdraw()
```

We change to `%pylab inline` because having all those widgets can actually cause a problem with Jupyter when you want to display a video sequence. We'll need the same code to get started with as shown in the previous example, and only replace `notebook` with `inline`. Then, we run the same code again.

After its execution, we move on with the next part. This is actually very close to the same thing because all you have to do is iterate over each frame, and it will work just the same:

```
predictor_path = "./shape_predictor_68_face_landmarks.dat"
detector = dlib.get_frontal_face_detector()
predictor = dlib.shape_predictor(predictor_path)
```

So, you see this code is pretty much the same as the previous example. If you want, you can do this with your webcam. It's actually pretty neat to watch. We'll not be using a webcam here, but for your custom project, if you want to use a webcam you can add the following line:

```
cap = cv2.VideoCapture(0)
#0 is the first camera on your computer, change if you have more #than one
camera
```

We're assuming here that you only have one webcam. If you have more than one camera and you don't want to use the first one, then you might need to change that 0 to something else. If you don't want to use your webcam, add the following line:

```
cap = cv2.Videocapture('./rollerc.mp4')
```

Here, we are not using a webcam. We want to create a figure that we're going to display, and we'll name it 100 to make sure it has its own unique ID. We'll use the same `font` as in the previous example:

```
font = cv2.FONT_HERSHEY_SIMPLEX
```

It sounds really complicated, but it's just an ordinary font. We're going to create a `while` loop, which is going to go over each and every frame:

```
while(True):
    #capture frame-by-frame
ret, img = cap.read
img.flags['WRITEABLE']=True #just in case
```

So, we have `cap` as our video capture object from OpenCV, and then all we have to do to read the frames is `cap.read()`. `ret` is just code that makes sure that we actually read a frame. Then, `img` is the actual image that is returned, and again make sure that the `WRITEABLE` flag is set, otherwise dlib could produce an error.

We're going to try to find a face and, if the face is not found, then we're going to release and break out of our loop:

```
try:
    dets = detector(img, 1)
    shape = predictor(img, dets[0])
except:
    print('no face detected', end='\r')
    cap.release()
    break
```

You might not want this for your application, but one neat thing here is if you're using a webcam, an easy way to just stop this loop from running indefinitely is to just put your hand in front of the face. You put your hand in front of the camera, or turn your head, or whatever, and that will automatically stop it, hands-free. Otherwise, you can send a kernel interrupt and just make sure you do `cap.release()`, otherwise the video source will stay open and you might get an error later.

According to the preceding code block, we grab the image, detect the faces, and take the shape. For this code, we'll assume that there's only one face, but you can see from the previous example how to deal with multiple faces.

Then, we create the blank image or the image that's a copy of the original, which we can write without distorting the original. Set the `head_width` and `fontsize`, and then just do exactly what we did before. Find the x and y points, and then write to them:

```
annotated=img.copy()
head_width = shape.part(16).x-shape.part(0).x
fontsize = head_width/650
for pt in range(68):
    x,y = shape.part(pt).x, shape.part(pt).y
    annotated=cv2.putText(annotated, str(pt), (x,y), font, fontsize,
(255,255,255),2, cv2.LINE_AA)
```

We are going to display our results, as shown in the following code:

```
fig=imshow(cv2.cvtColor(annotated, cv2.COLOR_BGR2RGB
```

Note the color, `BGR2RGB`. That's because OpenCV uses **blue green red** (**BGR**) by default, and the colors will look really funny if you don't change that for the display. Then, there's some stuff here that will make sure that our window is updating while the script is still running. Otherwise, it will actually just run the entire script and you won't see what's happening in real time.

We then hit *Shift + Enter*. It might take a second to load and then it'll run pretty slowly, largely because it's part of Jupyter Notebook. You can take the code out and run it as an independent program, and probably you'll want to create a `cv2` named window, but this will do for our purposes. When you execute the cell, you'll see two women:

One face is kind of obscured, so it's not going to detect her, but for the one who's in the foreground, as you can see, her face is being tracked pretty nicely and the landmarks are being found. This can work in real time depending on your hardware, and this isn't the kind of thing that you want to run in a Jupyter Notebook. You can watch this as long as you want to, but you get the idea.

So, that's how easy it is to work with video. Switch to the other woman in the background, and the first one's face is turned:

That's how easy it is to work with video, and you can detect multiple faces and do whatever you want with this information.

Facial recognition

We're going to see how we can perform facial recognition with dlib with a relatively small amount of code. Facial recognition here means that we're going to look at an image and see whether or not this person is the same as the person in a different image. We're going to keep it simple here and just compare two faces to see whether they're the same, but this can easily be generalized, as we'll see later.

Here, we're going to do something similar to the first example, where we're going to prompt the user to open two files, each with a face that is going to be compared to another. For this, we are going to use some faces from **Labeled Faces in the Wild (LFW)**. It's a nice database that has thousands of faces from various celebrities. You can download the entire set from `http://vis-www.cs.umass.edu/lfw/` and get a whole lot of examples that you can play with. So, we are just going to use a small subset of examples from the dataset to do our example here.

We prompt a user to select two different facial images. We're going to start the initial directory in the `faces` subdirectory of the project folder:

```
#Prompt the user for two images with one face each
imgname = filedialog.askopenfilename(parent=root, initialdir='faces',
title='First face...')
face1 = imread(imgname)
face1.flags['WRITEABLE']=True
#second face
imgname = filedialog.askopenfilename(parent=root, initialdir='faces',
title='Second face...')
face2 = imread(imgname)
face2.flags['WRITEABLE']=True
```

There are two additional files that you're going to need from `dlib.net/files`, and they are the `shape_predictor_5_face_landmarks.dat` file and the `dlib_face_recognition_resnet_model_v1.dat` file. Again, they're going to be in `bz2` format. So, interestingly, we're only using five facial landmarks for this, but combined with the descriptors that's actually very adequate for describing a human face. Hence, we are not using 68 face landmarks, but just 5. We'll see just how nicely that works. Download those files and unzip `bz2`, just as we did in the first example.

Now, we set the path to the proper file locations:

```
predictor_path = './shape_predictor_5_face_landmarks.dat
face_rec_model_path= './ dlib_face_recognition_resnet_model_v1.dat
```

The `predictor` works similarly to the 68 face landmarks, but again a link comes up with five results, and we're going to use a pre-trained recognition model. It works on a variety of faces; you won't have to retrain it now. Here, we don't have to do any complicated deep learning modeling for this. There are ways to train your own models, but you'll see that this will actually work very nicely for a wide variety of applications.

So, we create our `detector`, as before. That doesn't require any additional data:

```
detector = dlib.get_frontal_face_detector()
```

We're going to create our shape finder, similar to the previous example, and again we're using the five facial landmarks detector. We're going to create a new `facerec` object that comes from `dlib.face_recognition_model_v1`, passing in the path as `face_rec_model_path`:

```
sp = dlib.shape_predictor(predictor_path)
facerec = dlib.face_recognition_model_v1(face_rec_model_path)
```

Now, what `facerec` does is it takes a mapping, given our detected face and given the shapes and the location of where those landmarks are, and it's going to create a 128-length float vector, called a descriptor, that's going describe the face. So, it actually creates something that will be a description of a face, and is something that will capture the essence of a face. If you have the same person in two different pictures, where in one picture the person is far away from the camera and in another their face might be turned, it could be as many pictures and there could be different lighting conditions and so forth. The descriptor should be pretty much invariant to that. The descriptor is never exactly the same, but the same person should get a similar enough face descriptor, regardless of their orientation, the lighting conditions, and so forth. Even if they change their hair or they're wearing a hat, you should get a similar descriptor, and `facerec` actually does a good job of that.

The following code just performs the detection and the shape finding:

```
dets1 = detector(face1, 1)
shape1 = sp(face1, dets1[0])
dets2 = detector(face2, 1)
shape2 = sp(face2, dets2[0])
```

Then, we're going to perform the operation that we described previously: given the detection, spatial features, and the landmarks, we're going to compute the 128-point vector, and we can inspect it a little bit. Then, we're going to look at the faces side by side:

```
figure(200)
subplot(1,2,1)
imshow(face1)
subplot(1,2,2)
imshow(face2)
```

Now, we want to know how similar the faces are, so we're going to compute the Euclidean distance:

```
euclidean_distance = np.linalg.norm(np.array(face_descriptor1)-
np.array(face_descriptor2))
```

What that means is you take each point, 1 through 128, and you subtract the second one from the first one, you square each one, you sum them together, and take the square root, and that's going to give you a single number. That number is going to be used to determine whether or not these two images are of the same person's face.

There's a magic number, `0.6`, which we're going to use here, and which has been determined empirically to work very well. If the 128-dimensional distance is less than `0.6`, we say that these two images are of the same person. If it's more than `0.6`, or equal to `0.6` as in this case, we're going to say that these are different people. So, we look at the two images, compute all those metrics, and then we're going to say if it is <`0.6`, the faces match, and if it is >`0.6`, the faces are different:

```
if euclidean_distance<0.6:
    print('Faces match')
else:
    print('Faces are different')
```

Now, let's run the code. You'll see a dialog of celebrity photos from the LFW. We'll pick one of Alec Baldwin and one of Sylvester Stallone:

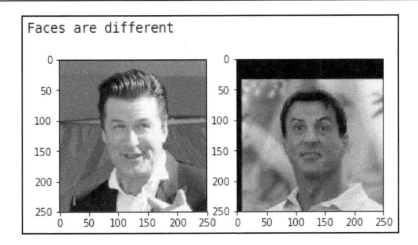

Baldwin and Sylvester Stallone are classified as two different people. That is exactly as we expected, as the faces are different. Now, let's do it for another pair. Let's compare Alec Baldwin to Alec Baldwin:

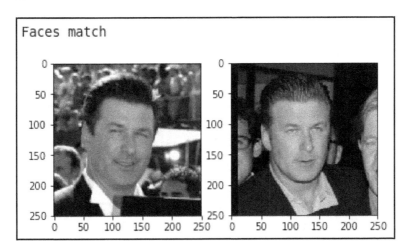

Here, you can see that their faces match. Let's do a few more comparisons for fun. So, Yao Ming and Winona Ryder look different from each other:

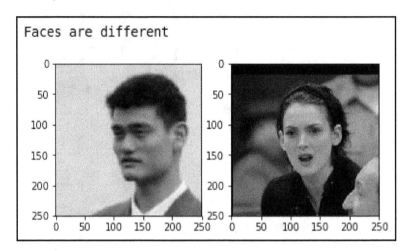

Then, we take two different pictures of Winona Ryder, and the faces match:

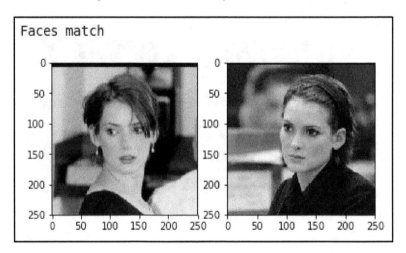

You can do all kinds of combinations of this. Okay, so this is pretty easy. It might be useful to take a look at the facial descriptor; you can just hit *Shift + Tab,* and you can see what the vectors look like, which is something like this:

```
Type:           vector
String form:
-0.147528
          0.048263
          0.0316406
          -0.124176
          -0.0820134
          -0.0260086
          -0.0338606
          -0.10674
          0.166148
          -0.1133 <...> 79
          0.114875
          -0.0459535
          -0.0619625
          -0.120842
          -0.0212056
          -0.0608454
          -0.101526
          0.0224088
```

It's not very human-understandable, but is available just in case you're curious about it. That is enough to capture the essence of a human face, and just using a simple comparison, we can actually do a pretty good job of telling whether the two pictures are of the same face. This actually has a greater than 99% accuracy on the LFW dataset. So, you'll actually have a difficult time finding two faces that get bad results, whether two faces of the same person that are said not to match, or two of different people that are said to match.

Therefore, if you wanted to adapt this to your own needs, what you can do is get your own database, just your own directory of faces of people that you want to recognize, and then when you have a new face, just go through each of the faces in your database. Just do a `for` loop and compare your new face to each one. For the Euclidean distance, computed here simply by using the NumPy linear algebra norm (`np.linalg.norm`), if that distance is less than 0.6, then you can say that you have a match. If you are concerned with false positives, you can have multiple faces of a person and compare to each one, then do a majority rule.

Otherwise, suppose you have ten faces and you want to make sure that all ten of them match. If you really want to make sure that you did not get a false positive, you can just get ten really good images and then compare your new test image to all ten. But in any case, you can see from this example that it does not take a whole lot of code, and this method can be adapted to a wide variety of applications.

Summary

In this chapter, we had a brief introduction to the dlib library and learned how to use it for facial recognition. We then learned how to generate the outline for a face using the 68 facial landmarks pre-trained model. Later, we learned how to find the facial landmarks for a single person, multiple people, and for people in videos.

In the next chapter, `Chapter 7`, *Deep Learning Image Classification with TensorFlow*, we'll learn how to classify images with TensorFlow using a pre-trained model, and later we'll use our own custom images.

7
Deep Learning Image Classification with TensorFlow

In this chapter, we will learn how to classify images using TensorFlow. First, we will use a pre-trained model, and then we'll proceed with training our own model using custom images.

Toward the end of the chapter, we will make use of the GPU to help us speed up our computations.

In this chapter, we will cover the following:

- A deep introduction to TensorFlow
- Using a pre-trained model (Inception) for image classification
- Retraining with our own images
- Speeding up computation with the GPU

Technical requirements

Along with knowledge of Python and the basics of image processing and computer vision, you will need the following libraries:

- TensorFlow
- NVIDIA CUDA® Deep Neural Network

The code used in the chapter has been added to the following GitHub repository:
`https://github.com/PacktPublishing/Computer-Vision-Projects-with-OpenCV-and-Python-3`

An introduction to TensorFlow

In this chapter, we'll go deeper into TensorFlow and see how we can build a general-purpose image classifier using its deep learning method.

This will be an extension of what we learned in `Chapter 2`, *Handwritten Digit Recognition with scikit-learn and TensorFlow*, where we learned how to classify handwritten digits. However, this method is quite a bit more powerful, as it will work on general images of people, animals, food, everyday objects, and so on.

To start, let's talk a little bit about what TensorFlow does, and the general workflow of TensorFlow.

To begin, what is a tensor? Wikipedia states this:

"In mathematics, tensors are geometric objects that describe linear relations between geometric vectors, scalars, and other tensors... Given a reference basis of vectors, a tensor can be represented as an organized multi-dimensional array of numerical values."

However, according to Google, the makers of TensorFlow, a tensor is any multi-dimensional array with any data type. Essentially, according to Google, a tensor can mean basically anything.

Google has generalized the word so much that it doesn't really mean a lot, and personally I don't like that (coming from an engineering and physics background). However, TensorFlow is so powerful and useful that I'm going to get over it. Just be aware that if you're ever worried about misusing the word *tensor*, don't be, because Google completely misuses it anyway.

For now, all we need to know is that within TensorFlow, a tensor is some sort of data; usually a multi-dimensional array, but it could be basically anything, such as images or text. With that in mind, TensorFlow is, in general, a high-performance numerical library. It is primarily geared toward machine learning, but that doesn't mean that it's exclusively made for machine learning.

TensorFlow can also be used for simulations, solving complex partial differential equations, and just about anything numerical. We're only concerned with machine learning and, in particular, deep learning in this chapter. We are going to be using it for its main purpose, but just be aware that it's generally used for constructing and analyzing complex numerical models.

Before we go into building a classifier, I want to share a little bit about how we would generally use TensorFlow for very basic usage. Start as follows:

1. We're going to change directories, and make sure that we can load key libraries and display images and so forth, using the following code:

```
#Get started with needed libraries/settings/directory
%pylab inline
%cd C:\Users\mrever\Documents\packt_CV\tensclass
```

2. Next, we import `tensorflow` and `numpy`, using the standard convention:

```
import tensorflow as tf
import numpy as np
```

Since we performed `pylab inline`, we don't explicitly need to import `numpy`, but it's a good practice in general. If we want to copy some of this code out to other scripts, we need to make sure that `numpy` is imported.

3. Let's start with a simple TensorFlow example. We're just going to perform some really basic arithmetic. Define some constants within TensorFlow, as follows:

```
#Arithmetic with TensorFlow

a = tf.constant(2)
b = tf.constant(3)
```

These constants can be just scalars, as we defined, or they could be vectors or matrices. We're just going to add them together. When we do that, we can define our constants.

4. We define constants, and then we create a TensorFlow session using the `with` clause. When it goes outside the `with` clause, we'll close the TensorFlow session, as follows:

```
with tf.Session() as sess:
    print("a=2, b=3")
    print("a+b=" + str(sess.run(a+b)))
    print("a*b=" + str(sess.run(a*b)))
```

 `Session` can be important depending on what resources we're using, for example, if we're using a GPU and we want to release it, but in this section, we're just going to be talking about the `Session` using the CPU.

Within our `Session`, TensorFlow has operator overloading where it makes sense. It understands what is meant by `a+b`, where `a` and `b` are both TensorFlow constants. It also understands arithmetic operations such as multiply (`*`), minus (–), divide (`/`), and so on.

5. Now, we're going to do the same thing using a different method, by creating `placeholder` variables, as follows:

```
a = tf.placeholder(tf.int16)
b = tf.placeholder(tf.int16)
```

Often, we need to construct our model. That's what TensorFlow is based on, it's basically an input-output model. So, we have our input, which could be numbers, images, words, or whatever. We generally need to find placeholders before we input our data, and then define and construct our model.

6. In our case, we're just defining addition, just as we would normally define it, as follows:

```
add = tf.add(a, b)
mul = tf.multiply(a, b)
```

This could be something more complex such as building a neural network, a **convolutional neural network** (**CNN**), and so on.

We'll see a bit of that momentarily, but for now we define our inputs, our model, our operations, and so on, and we create what is called a *graph*, which will take our inputs and map them to the desired outputs.

7. Similarly, we're going to create a `session`, and then we're going to run our operations:

```
with tf.Session() as sess:
    print("a+b=" + str(sess.run(add, feed_dict={a: 2, b: 3})))
    print("a*b=" + str(sess.run(mul, feed_dict={a: 2, b: 3})))
```

In this case, we have to tell it what the values are, and then it does exactly what we expect, as follows:

```
with tf.Session() as sess:
    print("a+b=" + str(sess.run(add, feed_dict={a: 2, b: 3})))
    print("a*b=" + str(sess.run(mul, feed_dict={a: 2, b: 3})))

a=2, b=3
a+b=5
a*b=6
a+b=5
```

Nothing too exciting—this is just so we understand a little bit about what TensorFlow is doing. We'll take advantage of some higher-level libraries for this chapter, but this is important if we want to go further in the future.

Similarly, we're going to do matrix multiplication. As mentioned earlier, the constants can be more than just scalars. In this case, we're defining matrices, a 2 by 2 matrix and a 2 by 1 matrix, using the following steps:

1. We define our matrices as follows:

```
#Matrix multiplication
matrix1 = tf.constant([[1., 2.],[9.0,3.14159]])
matrix2 = tf.constant([[3.],[4.]])
```

2. Then, we tell it to multiply matrices, as follows:

```
product = tf.matmul(matrix1, matrix2)
```

3. We create our session:

```
with tf.Session() as sess:
    result = sess.run(product)
    print(result)
```

Now we run it, and then print the results. The output is as follows:

```
#Matrix multiplication
matrix1 = tf.constant([[1., 2.],[9.0,3.14159]])
matrix2 = tf.constant([[3.],[4.]])

product = tf.matmul(matrix1, matrix2)

with tf.Session() as sess:
    result = sess.run(product)
    print(result)

[[11.     ]
 [39.56636]]
```

Again, very basic, but very important in the future. We're not going to define our full network in this lesson, because that's very complex and very time-consuming to execute, but just mention the general steps for creating our own CNN.

We're going to create what is known as layers, define our input, and then we create a bunch of layers and stack them together and define how they're connected. We then find the output layer and then we have to define some other things like how we're going to train and how we're going to evaluate it.

The code for this is as follows:

```
#creating a convolutional neural network (skeleton--not complete code!)

# create a convolutional (not fully connected) layer...
conv1 = tf.layers.conv2d(x, 32, 5, activation=tf.nn.relu)
# and down-sample
conv1 = tf.layers.max_pooling2d(conv1, 2, 2)

# create second layer
conv2 = tf.layers.conv2d(conv1, 64, 3, activation=tf.nn.relu)
conv2 = tf.layers.max_pooling2d(conv2, 2, 2)

# flatten to 1D
fc1 = tf.contrib.layers.flatten(conv2)

# create fully-connected layer
fc1 = tf.layers.dense(fc1, 1024)


# final (output/prediction) layer
```

```
out = tf.layers.dense(fc1, n_classes)

#...training code etc.
```

Again, this is just for our knowledge. Deep learning is a difficult subject, figuring out the necessary architecture and exactly how to train, which is beyond the scope of this chapter (although I would invite you to learn more about it). Here, we're just going to see how we can utilize what's already done—but if you want to go further, this is where you would start.

In the next section, we're going to see how to use a pre-trained model, Inception, to perform our image classification.

Using Inception for image classification

In this section, we're going to use a pre-trained model, Inception, from Google to perform image classification. We'll then move on and build our own model—or, at least do some retraining on the model in order to train on our own images and classify our own objects.

For now, we want to see what we can do with a model that's already trained, which would take a lot of time to reproduce from scratch. Let's get started with the code.

Let's go back to Jupyter Notebook. The Notebook file can be found at `https://github.com/PacktPublishing/Computer-Vision-Projects-with-OpenCV-and-Python-3/Chapter04`.

In order to run the code, we're going to need to download a file from TensorFlow's website, from the following link: `http://download.tensorflow.org/models/image/imagenet/inception-2015-12-05.tgz`. This is the Inception model.

The model was trained in 2015. It contains a couple of files that define the model, the *graph* as it is called, defining the input-output relation between the input images that we provide it and the output classification.

It also contains some labeling data because the output isn't class names; it is numbers. This is modified from Google own TensorFlow's example, to make it easier to understand and run in Jupyter Notebook and reduce the amount of code. However, we need to change that.

Get the file and completely unzip it. On Windows, readers might use 7-Zip, which will give a TGZ file. Make sure to then untar the TGZ file to get the TXT, PBTXT, and PB files, particularly the PB file, as that is the one that actually contains the trained model.

We create a file called `inceptiondict`, rather than using Google's own convoluted file for mapping the class numbers to the class name.

Let's take a look at the `inceptiondict` file:

```
inception_1000_class_list.txt
  1   {0: 'tench, Tinca tinca',
  2    1: 'goldfish, Carassius auratus',
  3    2: 'great white shark, white shark, man-eater, man-eating shark, Carcharodon carcharias',
  4    3: 'tiger shark, Galeocerdo cuvieri',
  5    4: 'hammerhead, hammerhead shark',
  6    5: 'electric ray, crampfish, numbfish, torpedo',
  7    6: 'stingray',
  8    7: 'cock',
  9    8: 'hen',
 10    9: 'ostrich, Struthio camelus',
 11   10: 'brambling, Fringilla montifringilla',
 12   11: 'goldfinch, Carduelis carduelis',
 13   12: 'house finch, linnet, Carpodacus mexicanus',
 14   13: 'junco, snowbird',
 15   14: 'indigo bunting, indigo finch, indigo bird, Passerina cyanea',
 16   15: 'robin, American robin, Turdus migratorius',
 17   16: 'bulbul',
 18   17: 'jay',
 19   18: 'magpie',
 20   19: 'chickadee',
 21   20: 'water ouzel, dipper',
 22   21: 'kite',
 23   22: 'bald eagle, American eagle, Haliaeetus leucocephalus',
 24   23: 'vulture',
 25   24: 'great grey owl, great gray owl, Strix nebulosa',
 26   25: 'European fire salamander, Salamandra salamandra',
 27   26: 'common newt, Triturus vulgaris',
 28   27: 'eft',
 29   28: 'spotted salamander, Ambystoma maculatum',
 30   29: 'axolotl, mud puppy, Ambystoma mexicanum',
 31   30: 'bullfrog, Rana catesbeiana',
```

This file has a thousand classes. It would take a very long time to train this yourself, but we don't have to; we can take advantage of this and build off it, as we'll see later.

This file is interesting to look at if we want to know what kinds of images we'll be able to recognize within this pre-built model. There are a lot of animals in the file, some common items, fruits, musical instruments, different kinds of fish; it even recognizes the Japanese game *shoji,* apparently.

We're going to import this file as a dictionary called `inceptiondict`, which will map numbers to their corresponding class descriptions; for example, class 1 maps to the description `"goldfish, Carassius auratus"`.

Let's explore the main code. Firstly, we import the file as `inceptiondict`:

```
#The main code:
#"image" is a filename for the image we want to classify

#load our inception-id to English description dictionary
from inceptiondict import inceptiondict
```

Now, we have our `run_inference_on_image` function, where `image` is a filename. It is not the file data—we haven't loaded that yet—just the filename for the image that we want to classify.

Then, we check to make sure that filename exists, and create an error if it doesn't. If it does exist, then we use TensorFlow's own loading mechanism in order to read that filename, as follows:

```
def run_inference_on_image(image):

    #load image (making sure it exists)
    if not tf.gfile.Exists(image):
        tf.logging.fatal('File does not exist %s', image)
    image_data = tf.gfile.FastGFile(image, 'rb').read()
```

We were talking about the graph file before. Unzip the the crucial `classify_image_graph_def.pb` file from the TGZ file to the current directory. Open that as a binary by using TensorFlow's own file loading mechanism, and then we're going to create our graph definition from that, as follows:

```
# Load our "graph" file--
# This graph is a pretrained model that maps an input image
# to one (or more) of a thousand classes.
# Note: generating such a model from scratch is VERY computationally
# expensive
with tf.gfile.FastGFile('classify_image_graph_def.pb', 'rb') as f:
    graph_def = tf.GraphDef()
    graph_def.ParseFromString(f.read())
    _ = tf.import_graph_def(graph_def, name='')
```

Here, we are just loading the pre-trained model. Google already did the hard work for us, and we're going to read from that.

Then, as we did previously, we need to create our TensorFlow session. We do that with the `with` clause, as follows:

```
#create a TF session to actually apply our model
  with tf.Session() as sess:
      # Some useful tensors:
```

```
            # 'softmax:0': A tensor containing the normalized prediction across
            # 1000 labels.
            # 'pool_3:0': A tensor containing the next-to-last layer containing
 2048
            # float description of the image.
            # 'DecodeJpeg/contents:0': A tensor containing a string providing
 JPEG
            # encoding of the image.
            # Runs the softmax tensor by feeding the image_data as input to the
 graph.
            softmax_tensor = sess.graph.get_tensor_by_name('softmax:0')
            predictions = sess.run(softmax_tensor,
                            {'DecodeJpeg/contents:0': image_data})
            predictions = np.squeeze(predictions)
            #The output here is a 1000 length vector, each element between 0
 and 1,
            #that sums to 1. Each element may be thought of as a probability
            #that the image corresponds to a given class (object type, e.g.
 bird,
            #plane, and so on).
```

This model already has multiple layers called tensors. We need to extract the `softmax` layer.

The output of our model isn't just going to be that something was detected 100%; what it does is give a probability for each one. We might have, for example, a 90% probability that our image is some sort of cat, a 20% probability that it's a squirrel, and 0.01% that it's a chair or something. Yes, you do get some wild classifications sometimes, although typically those probabilities are very small.

Some fraction of probability is calculated for each one of the thousand classes. Of course, the vast majority of them are going to be zero or very, very close to zero.

We want to extract the next-to-last layer, containing 2048 close descriptions of the image and the input image that provides the JPEG encoding of the image. Note that we didn't load the raw image data in a two-dimensional or three-dimensional vector (or tensor as they call it)—we still have it in JPEG encoding. We're just defining our variables to extract the outputs and find the inputs.

NumPy's `squeeze` gets rid of all singleton dimensions. So, if we have a 1 by 1000, this will convert it to a 1000 by 1.

Okay, so, we understand the inputs and outputs within our session. Just for understanding's sake, we only want to extract the top five predictions, and we're going to filter out predictions that have a probability of less than 10%. At most, we're going to get five predictions, but it usually will be less as we disregard anything below 10%, as follows:

```
#We only care about the top 5 (at most) predictions, and ones that have
#at least a 10% probability of a match
num_top_predictions= 5
top_k = predictions.argsort()[-num_top_predictions:][::-1]
for node_id in top_k:
    human_string = inceptiondict[node_id]
    score = predictions[node_id]
    if score > 0.1:
        print('%s (score = %.5f)' % (human_string, score))
```

We run the model and get the output of the image, and then we sort by our top five. We then iterate over those top predictions and convert to a human string by running the output's `node_id` through our `inceptiondict` dictionary. We read the `score`, and then we only print the output if the `score` is greater than 10%.

We're just defining the function, we're not running it, so this should be instantaneous to run.

Now, we're going to run this on some images. There are some sample images in a `sample_imgs` subdirectory. What we want do is test this, so just uncomment out one of these following lines to define our `image` variable:

```
#uncomment out one of these lines to test

image='sample_imgs/cropped_panda.jpg'
# image='sample_imgs/dog.jpg'
# image='sample_imgs/bicycle2.jpg'
# image='sample_imgs/garbagecan.jpg'
# image='sample_imgs/bunny.jpg'
# image='sample_imgs/trombone.jpg'
# image='sample_imgs/treasurechest.jpg'
# image='sample_imgs/hotdog.jpg'
figure()
imshow(imread(image))
run_inference_on_image(image)
```

Then, we're going to create a figure, look at what we see using the `imshow` function, and then use the `run_inference_on_image` function, which will output the results.

To run the preceding block of code with our `cropped_panda.jpg` picture, uncomment the panda picture line. We can see the picture in the following output. It has classified it with about 90% probability as a `panda`, `giant panda`, or other synonym, as follows:

Let's try it on something else. How about our `bicycle2.jpg` file? Uncomment the `bicycle2.jpg` line while commenting back the `cropped_panda.jpg` line, and we get the following output:

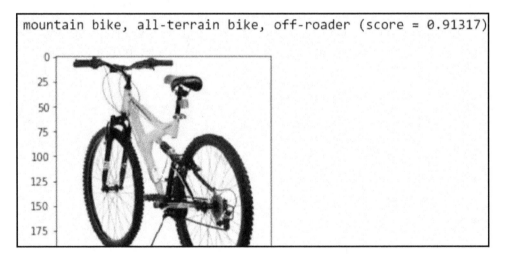

It has classified the picture with 91% probability as a `mountain bike`.

We are getting a little specific here. Let's try now with the `garbagecan.jpg` file:

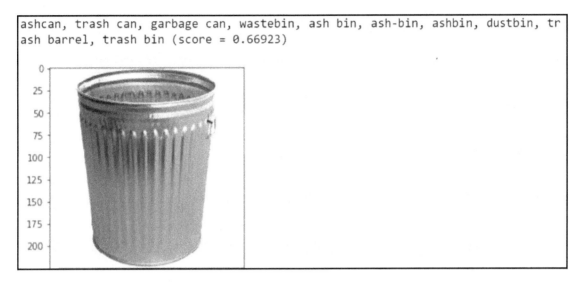

It wasn't as confident here, only about 67% probability in its classification. Sometimes that's the best we can do, but that's not too bad. That was the most likely result.

Let's try the `bunny.jpg` file:

Alright, 87% probability that we have a rabbit. Looks pretty good.

Now, let's try the `trombone.jpg` file:

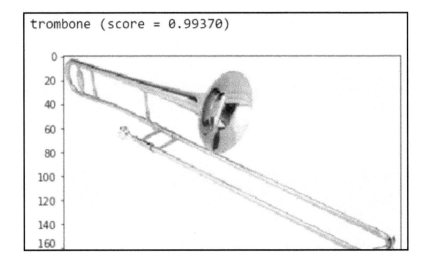

Wow, very certain. Over 99% probability that the picture is of a `trombone`—very good.

If you're a fan of a certain popular TV show, you might be wondering whether the classifier can recognize a hot dog. The answer to that is yes:

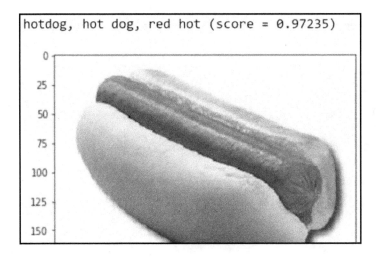

It does recognize a `hotdog`, with 97% confidence.

Finally, we're going to run our classifier on `dog.jpg`, as follows:

Whoever trained this model was apparently a dog lover, so they defined a bunch of different dog classes. We get `Irish wolfhound`, `Russian wolfhound`, `gazelle hound`, and others returned. It seems to think that it's one of those!

This is working pretty well. If what we need happens to fall within those 1,000 classes, then we're in good shape here. You should be able to adapt the code in the Jupyter Notebook to your needs. Hopefully, deep learning and image classification don't seem quite as intimidating as they did before.

So, with that, we're going to move on to the next section, where we do some retraining with our own images and classify objects that are not already in Google's training database.

Retraining with our own images

In this section, we're going to go beyond what we did with the pre-built classifier and use our own images with our own labels.

The first thing I should mention is that this isn't really training from scratch with deep learning—there are multiple layers and algorithms for training the whole thing, which are very time-consuming—but we can take advantage of something called *transfer learning*, where we take the first few layers that were trained with a very large number of images, as illustrated in the following diagram:

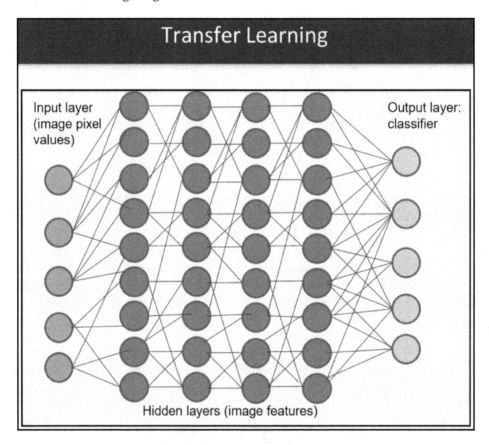

It's one of the caveats of deep learning that having a few hundred or a few thousand images isn't enough. You need hundreds of thousands or even millions of samples in order to get good results, and gathering that much data is very time-consuming. Also, running it on a personal computer, which I expect most people are using, is not computationally feasible.

But the good news is that we can take layers from our pre-existing model and just do some tweaking at the end, and get some very good results. We're taking advantage of the pre-training by using input features that were trained on hundreds of thousands or millions of images, and transferring them to image types that the model has never seen before.

To do this, we borrow some code from TensorFlow Hub (`https://www.tensorflow.org/hub/`). But we have to make some tweaks to make it run more easily with reduced code and make it so that we can just drop it into our Jupyter Notebook and run it.

In order to get started, we need some images on which to train, and different ways of doing that. Google has kindly provided a sample called `flower_photos` at the following link: `http://download.tensorflow.org/example_images/flower_photos.tgz`. Once again, it's a TGZ file, so download the file and thoroughly unzip it.

You'll get a `flower_photos` directory, which will contain some subdirectories of different kinds of flowers such as tulips, dandelions, and so on, which were not among the 1,000 original classes. Those directory names will serve as the labels for those images. All we have to do is unzip them and then input flower photos in the our code.

A cheap method to get a whole lot of photos is to use the Fatkun Batch Download plugin for Chrome (`https://chrome.google.com/webstore/detail/fatkun-batch-download-ima/nnjjahlikiabnchcpehcpkdeckfgnohf?hl=en`). Using this, we can go somewhere like Google Image Search and search for whatever kind of object we want—animal, food, and so on—and grab hundreds of images pretty quickly.

There are similar plugins for Firefox, or whatever web browser you are using. As long as you don't mind using those kinds of images, if they will suit your needs then this is a good way to do it.

After you're finished with the flower photos, I would suggest grabbing your own images. Think of something that you'd like to train on, something that you think would be useful. Try to get at least 100 images of each class and grab multiple classes.

For illustration purposes, I decided to classify some toys. Maybe you're running a toy store and you're taking inventory, or you're a collector and you want to know what exactly is in there—you just have a bunch of photos, and you want to classify them.

I created four subfolders called `barbie`, `gi joe`, `my little pony`, and `transformers`, shown as follows:

barbie	12/20/2018 11:17 …	File folder
gi joe	12/20/2018 11:17 …	File folder
my little pony	12/20/2018 11:17 …	File folder
transformers	12/20/2018 11:21 …	File folder

Each folder contains over 100 images of each type. The filenames are not important—just the directory names are going to be used for the labeling.

So you can test whether or not it's working, you need to separate out some images. If you test on images that you trained on, then you're kind of cheating—you don't really know whether or not your model has generalized. So, make sure to pull out some images from that directory and put them in a separate directory for now.

The code for retraining is introduced in the Jupyter Notebook file itself, so we're not going to go through the whole thing. We've created a file called `retrained.py`, which is based on the TensorFlow Hub version, but is more easily dropped into existing code and a lot of the variables are already taken care of.

All we need to do is import the `retrain` function, and then we retrain on our `toy_images` folder, as follows:

```
#pull the function from our custom retrain.py file
from retrain import retrain

#Now we'll train our model and generate our model/graph file
'output_graph.pb'
retrain('toy_images')
```

This generally takes a while. If you run the code on the `flower_photos` directory, that will take about half an hour, especially if doing it on a CPU and not a GPU. The `toy_images` example will take a little less time, because there aren't as many images.

Training in general with machine learning is the time-consuming portion; that's what's going to tie up your computer for long periods. Running images through a classifier is quick, as we saw before, but training can take minutes, hours, days, or possibly even longer. In this case, we're looking at up to half an hour, depending on how many images are present.

After a couple of minutes, our `retrained` function has run successfully, with the following output:

```
#pull the function from our custom retrain.py file
from retrain import retrain

#Now we'll train our model and generate our model/graph file 'output_graph.pb'
retrain('toy_images')

Retraining with images in directory: toy_images
Converted 378 variables to const ops.
```

I've turned down some of the verbosity in the retrain function, as otherwise it spits out a lot of messages that don't mean much. You can go into the code if you want and turn that up, if you're concerned it's not running successfully, but it should run just fine as long as everything's set up correctly.

Let's confirm that it works:

```
#Confirm that it worked
!ls *.pb

#should see file "output_graph.pb"
```

We're going to look for that .pb file (Python binary file), which will be the output of what we did. So, that's the model, the input-output model, or graph as it's typically called in TensorFlow.

After running the code, we should get the following output:

```
#Confirm that it worked
!ls *.pb

#should see file "output_graph.pb

classify_image_graph_def.pb
output_graph - Copy.pb
output_graph.pb
```

We have this file called output_graph.pb. That's the one we just created; you should see this file in your directory.

The code for running your images isn't quite as complicated. Loading our output_graph.pb graph file is similar to what we did before when we loaded the Inception model, as follows:

```
#Let's load some code that will run our model on a specified image

def load_graph(model_file):
    graph = tf.Graph()
    graph_def = tf.GraphDef()

    with open(model_file, "rb") as f:
        graph_def.ParseFromString(f.read())
    with graph.as_default():
        tf.import_graph_def(graph_def)

    return graph
```

The `read_tensor_from_image_file` function helps in reading data from the image file, as follows:

```python
def read_tensor_from_image_file(file_name,
                                input_height=299,
                                input_width=299,
                                input_mean=0,
                                input_std=255):
    input_name = "file_reader"
    output_name = "normalized"
    file_reader = tf.read_file(file_name, input_name)
    if file_name.endswith(".png"):
        image_reader = tf.image.decode_png(
                file_reader, channels=3, name="png_reader")
    elif file_name.endswith(".gif"):
        image_reader = tf.squeeze(
                tf.image.decode_gif(file_reader, name="gif_reader"))
    elif file_name.endswith(".bmp"):
        image_reader = tf.image.decode_bmp(file_reader, name="bmp_reader")
    else:
        image_reader = tf.image.decode_jpeg(
                file_reader, channels=3, name="jpeg_reader")
    float_caster = tf.cast(image_reader, tf.float32)
    dims_expander = tf.expand_dims(float_caster, 0)
    resized = tf.image.resize_bilinear(dims_expander, [input_height,
input_width])
    normalized = tf.divide(tf.subtract(resized, [input_mean]), [input_std])
    sess = tf.Session()
    result = sess.run(normalized)

    return result
```

There are some defaults here, but they don't matter. Images don't necessarily need to be 299 by 299. We're just dealing with JPEGs here, but if we have files in PNG, GIF, or BMP formats, the model can handle that. We just decode the images, put them into our variable, and store and return them.

As said before, the labels come from the directories. The following code will load the created `output_labels.txt` it's going to load it from `output_labels.txt`, and that's going to be our dictionary of sorts, as defined by our subdirectory names:

```
def load_labels(label_file):
    label = []
    proto_as_ascii_lines = tf.gfile.GFile(label_file).readlines()
    for l in proto_as_ascii_lines:
        label.append(l.rstrip())
    return label
```

The following code shows the `label_image` function. To find an image you know, give the correct filename, but there is a default just in case:

```
def label_image(file_name=None):
    if not file_name:
        file_name = "test/mylittlepony2.jpg"
    model_file = "./output_graph.pb"
    label_file = "./output_labels.txt"
    input_height = 299
    input_width = 299
    input_mean = 0
    input_std = 255
    input_layer = "Placeholder"
    output_layer = "final_result"
```

I have hardcoded these in for simplicity. If you want to change stuff, you can, but I think that having it written there makes things easy to read and understand.

We load our graph file, read our data from the image file, and read layer names from the new model that we created, as follows:

```
graph = load_graph(model_file)
t = read_tensor_from_image_file(
        file_name,
        input_height=input_height,
        input_width=input_width,
        input_mean=input_mean,
        input_std=input_std)

input_name = "import/" + input_layer
output_name = "import/" + output_layer
input_operation = graph.get_operation_by_name(input_name)
output_operation = graph.get_operation_by_name(output_name)
```

We're just going to read the input and output layers.

We define our session and get our results from `output_operation`. Again, we sort it to the `top_k` variable, and print the results:

```
with tf.Session(graph=graph) as sess:
    results = sess.run(output_operation.outputs[0], {
            input_operation.outputs[0]: t
    })
results = np.squeeze(results)

top_k = results.argsort()[-5:][::-1]
labels = load_labels(label_file)
for i in top_k:
    print(labels[i], results[i])
```

There are a lot of classes, but we're actually going to see it's always just going to be one result here.

Let's try our code again. As discussed, we separated a couple of images out into a separate directory, because we don't want to test on our training images, as that proves nothing.

Let's test the retrained model on our first `transformers1.jpg` image. The model is to display the image and tell us what the classification results were:

```
#label_image will load our test image and tell us what class/type it is

#uncomment one of these lines to test
#
test_image='test/transformers1.jpg'
# test_image='test/transformers2.jpg'
# test_image='test/transformers3.jpg'

# test_image='test/mylittlepony1.jpg'
# test_image='test/mylittlepony2.jpg'
# test_image='test/mylittlepony3.jpg'

# test_image='test/gijoe1.jpg'
# test_image='test/gijoe2.jpg'
# test_image='test/gijoe3.jpg'

# test_image='test/barbie1.jpg'
# test_image='test/barbie2.jpg'
# test_image='test/barbie3.jpg'

#display the image
figure()
```

```
imshow(imread(test_image))

#and tell us what the classification result is
label_image(test_image)
```

The output for the preceding code is as follows:

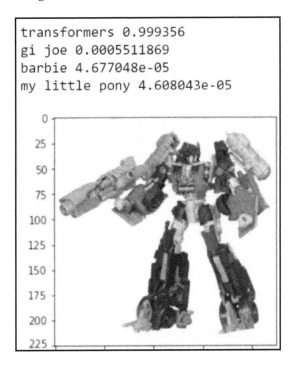

The model classified the image with a very high probability that this was a transformers.
Since our images are distinct enough, and there are fewer classes, it's going to work very
nicely. We see there is a 99.9% probability the picture is of a Transformer, a small
probability that it is a GI Joe, and it's most definitely not a Barbie or a My Little Pony.

We can use *Ctrl* + / to comment and uncomment lines in the code in Jupyter Notebook, and press *Ctrl* + *Enter* to run the code again with the `transformer2.jpg` picture:

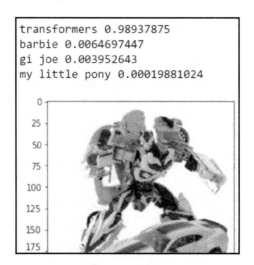

The output is `transformers` again. This time the model thinks it is slightly more likely to be a Barbie than a GI Joe, but the probability is insignificant.

Let's try again with the `mylittlepony1.jpg` picture:

And yes, it definitely looks like other images in the my little pony subfolder.

Let's take another picture, mylittlepony3.jpg:

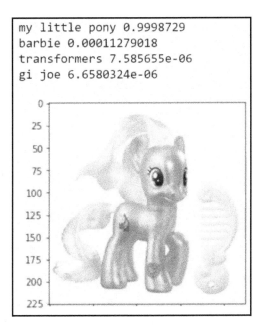

```
my little pony 0.9998729
barbie 0.00011279018
transformers 7.585655e-06
gi joe 6.6580324e-06
```

Again, no problem classifying the image. Let's take a look at gijoe2.jpg too:

```
gi joe 0.9767354
transformers 0.020028114
barbie 0.0028766098
my little pony 0.00035978633
```

There's a high probability of it being a `gi joe`, `transformers` and `barbie` are more likely than `my little pony`, but again all those probabilities are insignificant—it's definitely a `gi joe`.

Finally, let's try it on `barbie1.jpg`:

```
barbie 0.99953246
my little pony 0.0002746276
transformers 0.00013877105
gi joe 5.407119e-05
```

Again, definitely classified as a `barbie`, and `my little pony` was the second most likely, perhaps because of the colors; there tends to be more pink and purple on Barbie and My Little Pony toys.

Now we know how we can use our own images to retrain a pre-existing model. With not a lot of coding or CPU time, we can create a custom image classifier for our own purposes.

In the next section, we're going to talk about speeding up the computations with the help of your GPU.

Speeding up computation with your GPU

In this section, we'll talk briefly about speeding up computations with your GPU. The good news is that TensorFlow is actually very smart about using the GPU, so if you have everything set up, then it's pretty simple.

Let's see what things look like if we have the GPU properly set up. First, import TensorFlow as follows:

```
import tensorflow
```

Next, we print `tensorflow.Session()`. This just gives us information about our CPU and GPU (if it is properly set up):

```
print(tensorflow.Session())
```

The output is as follows:

```
In [2]: print(tensorflow.Session())
2018-04-29 23:40:34.654575: I T:\src\github\tensorflow\tensorflow\core\platform\cpu_feature_guard.cc:140] Your CPU supports instructions that
this TensorFlow binary was not compiled to use: AVX2
2018-04-29 23:40:35.152570: I T:\src\github\tensorflow\tensorflow\core\common_runtime\gpu\gpu_device.cc:1356] Found device 0 with properties:
name: GeForce GTX 970M major: 5 minor: 2 memoryClockRate(GHz): 1.038
pciBusID: 0000:01:00.0
totalMemory: 6.00GiB freeMemory: 4.90GiB
```

As we can see from the output, we're using a laptop with a GeForce GTX 970M, which is CUDA-compatible. This is needed in order to run TensorFlow with the GPU. If everything is set up properly, you will see a message very similar to the preceding output for your GPU, your card model, and details about it such as its memory and so forth.

TensorFlow is smart about it. We can override it ourselves, but that's only a good idea if we know what we're doing and we're willing to put in the extra work. Unless we know what we're doing, we're not going to get improved performance, so just leave the default settings.

Subsequent sections will run just fine on a CPU, just not quite as fast.

The bad news about TensorFlow using the GPU is that setting it up isn't quite as straightforward. We previously covered the `pip` command, for example, `pip install tensorflow` and `pip install tensorflow-gpu`, which is a starting point, but we'll still need CUDA to be installed.

I have version 9.0 installed. If you have a Quadro GPU or some sort of workstation, Tesla, or one of those specialized cards, you should use CUDA version 9.1. It's platform-dependent, depending on what kind of GPU you have and, more particularly, what kind of operating system, so we can't go into full details here.

What's important to know is that we can't just install `tensorflow-gpu`; we have to install CUDA. Download and install CUDA for your operating system from the NVIDIA website (`https://developer.nvidia.com/cuda-toolkit`).

In addition to that, TensorFlow requires the **NVIDIA CUDA® Deep Neural Network (cuDNN)** library, which is a big DLL file for Windows, or a shared object (`.SO`) file for Linux. It's similar for macOS as well. It's just one file, which needs to be in your path. I generally copy it over to my `CUDA` directory.

If you do have one, try to install CUDA, do try to install cuDNN, and try to get TensorFlow working. Hopefully, that will speed up computations for you.

Summary

In this chapter, we learned how to classify images using a pre-trained model based on TensorFlow. We then retrained our model to work with custom images.

Finally, we had a brief overview of how to speed up the classification process by carrying out the computation on a GPU.

Using the examples covered in this book, you will be able to carry your our custom projects using Python, OpenCV, and TensorFlow.

Other Books You May Enjoy

If you enjoyed this book, you may be interested in these other books by Packt:

Deep Learning for Computer Vision
Rajalingappaa Shanmugamani

ISBN: 978-1-78829-562-8

- Set up an environment for deep learning with Python, Tensorflow, and Keras
- Define and train a model for image and video classification
- Use features from a pre-trained Convolutional Neural Network model for image retrieval
- Understand and implement object detection using the real-world Pedestrian Detection scenario
- Learn about various problems in image captioning and how to overcome them by training images and text together
- Implement similarity matching and train a model for face recognition
- Understand the concept of generative models and use them for image generation
- Deploy your deep learning models and optimize them for high performance

Practical Computer Vision
Abhinav Dadhich

ISBN: 978-1-78829-768-4

- Learn the basics of image manipulation with OpenCV
- Implement and visualize image filters such as smoothing, dilation, histogram equalization, and more
- Set up various libraries and platforms, such as OpenCV, Keras, and Tensorflow, in order to start using computer vision, along with appropriate datasets for each chapter, such as MSCOCO, MOT, and Fashion-MNIST
- Understand image transformation and downsampling with practical implementations.
- Explore neural networks for computer vision and convolutional neural networks using Keras
- Understand working on deep-learning-based object detection such as Faster-R-CNN, SSD, and more
- Explore deep-learning-based object tracking in action
- Understand Visual SLAM techniques such as ORB-SLAM

Leave a review - let other readers know what you think

Please share your thoughts on this book with others by leaving a review on the site that you bought it from. If you purchased the book from Amazon, please leave us an honest review on this book's Amazon page. This is vital so that other potential readers can see and use your unbiased opinion to make purchasing decisions, we can understand what our customers think about our products, and our authors can see your feedback on the title that they have worked with Packt to create. It will only take a few minutes of your time, but is valuable to other potential customers, our authors, and Packt. Thank you!

Index

K

k-nearest neighbors (k-nn) 48
k-nearest neighbors digit classifier 48
kernels, plate utility functions
  blackhat, using 46
  graytop, using 46
  tophat, using 46

L

Labeled Faces in the Wild (LFW) 132
libraries
  installing 9
license plate
  identifying 43, 44
license plates, with OpenCV
  finding 54, 57
  reading 54, 57
  result analysis 57, 60, 62
long short-term memory (LSTM) 23

M

matching character function 46, 47
MNIST digit data
  acquiring 85, 87, 90, 92
  processing 85, 87, 90, 92
morphological functions 46
MPII Human Pose Models
  reference 65
multi-person pose detection 75, 78, 79, 81

N

NVIDIA CUDA® Deep Neural Network (cuDNN)
  166
NVIDIA
  reference 166

O

OpenCV
  installing 9
own images
  retraining 153, 155, 157, 160, 163, 164

P

plate characters
  finding 48, 51, 52
  groups, finding 52, 54
  matches, finding 52, 54
plate utility functions
  about 45
  gray_thresh_img function 46
  k-nearest neighbors digit classifier 48
  kernels 46
  matching character function 46, 47
  morphological functions 46
pose estimation
  ArtTrack, using 63, 65
  DeeperCut, using 63, 65
Python
  about 6
  installing 6

R

Recurrent neural networks (RNNs) 23
  with long short-term memory 22, 23
red green blue (RGB) 50
results
  evaluating 113, 115

S

single-person pose detection 66, 68, 71, 73, 75
support vector machine
  applying to new data 98
  applying, to new data 93, 96, 101, 104
  creating 92, 93
  training 92, 93

T

TensorFlow Hub
  reference 155
TensorFlow
  about 140, 142
  installing 11, 12
  with digit classification 104, 106, 111, 112
Tesseract
  installing 10, 11

V

www.ingramcontent.com/pod-product-compliance
Lightning Source LLC
LaVergne TN
LVHW081526050326
832903LV00025B/1653